Just Add Water

Jay Walden

ISBN-10: 1484067339
ISBN-13: 978-1484067338

FOREWORD

When I was a student at the University of Chicago, I took a course with a professor in the graduate school of English, Norman Maclean. The course wasn't about fishing, it was about Custer and the battle of the Little Big Horn. A few years later, Norman Maclean wrote "A River Runs Through It". In it he wrote that in his family there was no clear line between fly fishing and religion. I wasn't yet a fisherman nor was I religious. Then, settling in a small town near the Jemez Mountains of New Mexico I began to fish. I also had a secret life, a wonderful young girl friend I would sneak off to see in Albuquerque. And when, often in the wee hours of the morning, I did this, I would say "I'm going fishing." One morning just as dawn was breaking, my car reached an intersection near my home. One road went south, towards Albuquerque and that young girl. The other way went west, towards the Jemez mountains. As part of my cover I had all my fishing gear with me in the car. Then it hit me. I was torn. I actually wanted to go fishing.

Jay Walden lives in a small house behind Abe's Fly Shop. The San Juan River flows by, a few hundred yards away. There is something so intimate, so powerful, about the experience of fishing, that it becomes very problematic to share information. If the San Juan River was located in New Zealand I would tell you it was in Australia. But the San Juan River is not in New Zealand. It comes out from beneath a massive earth fill dam, and slowly moves through a flat desert valley, creating for the first few miles, one of the great trout fishing waters of North America. Jay doesn't just live in a little unit behind the fly shop. He spends over a hundred days a year, on the water. When he is not fishing he works behind the counter at Abe's. Roger works there too. Over the years it was Roger who taught me how to fish the river. If you mention using streamers to Roger he says things like "too much work."

One day Roger said he had a day off and I could go fishing with him. I was very excited. When I met Roger at the parking lot, I right away noticed Jay was there also. "What's he doing here?" I thought. Then Roger said, "don't mind Jay, he dry fly fishes, ants and hoppers" as if this put Jay into some sub category of human being, neither above nor below us, just different. Then the three of us went splashing up the trail, going through shallow water in order to reach where ever we were going. Only Jay never got there. At the side of a long flat pool, not a foot deep anywhere, Jay had moved off by himself. The air was still, the water like a mirror. I made a picture of Jay that morning. He seemed to be bent over at a right angle staring straight out across the water like a bird dog. Then he casted, a long straight effortless cast that went straight out in front of him. Nothing happened. Then he cast again. This time Jay caught the fish.

I've always been curious about what was inside Jay's little house behind Abe's, beyond his ninety pound Alsatian that lives behind the chain link fence out front in the yard. I've never been inside the house, but I image there is nothing much in there. It's why I like staying at Abe's motel. There is nothing in the rooms. Just some pegs to put up your rod, and hooks to hang your waders. The reason I think Jay's home is empty is because Jay lives to fish. In that sense Jay Walden is not quite right. He lives to be on the water. To be left alone, away from what we call civilization, away from other fisherman, in water, feeling the air, watching the swallows, looking for trout, tying on his hopper, throwing his ant, and watching the swirl, the breaking water, the San Juan rainbow, that magnificent swimming beast, ripping line, leaping in the air, heavy on his line.

Danny Lyon

Danny Lyon is author of The Bikeriders, soon to be re- issued by Aperture Publishers, New York, and Indian Nations, Twin Palms, Santa Fe. His next publication is a photographic memoir, The Seventh Dog, Phaidon Press Limited. His writing appears regularly on the blog Dektol.wordpress.com.

CONTENTS

Jay Walden

ACKNOWLEDGMENTS

I would first and foremost like to thank all of those faithful readers that have followed my fishing reports over the past several years, especially those who encouraged me to put them in book form. They planted the seed; for this, my first book. This endeavor was somewhat daunting; to say the least, not just because I had to bare my soul a bit in the poems and short stories that I decided to include, but also because I had to open my writing ability; or lack thereof, to the scrutiny of the whole wide world.

I'm indebted to Billy Foote, Glen Tinnin, and Danny Lyon, artists and writers; themselves, who provided me enough advice and affirmation to garner the courage to see this thing through, I would also like to acknowledge those who did all the heavy lifting that I couldn't, or wouldn't do, on my own. Judy Castle for her editing efforts, Paul Zimmerman from Aspire Computer Solutions that spent hours formatting and formulating pages and pages of documents into readable book form. Tim Martinez, for his time, patience, and tenacity in getting the photographic work, just right. Abe, Patsy, Tim and Andrea Chavez for offering me a venue to reach my readers.

Finally, a special thanks to my good friend and former fishing partner, Andrew Baca, who inspired me to seek out more adventure in my fly fishing pursuits. While some turned out to be a little more adventurous than we had initially bargained for, they sure made great material for some storytelling. To the Good Lord Above, thanks for letting me survive them and live long enough to share them with others.

Spring

1 SPRING

Wind

The winter had been colder than usual and each passing day only made Jay more certain that it was going to be summer, long before it was ever spring, this year. The wind had blown incessantly since March, the kind of wind that could drive a person batshit, especially a dry fly fisherman. No amount of wishing or hoping would change this weather, so he found himself rod in one hand, fly poised between forefinger and thumb in the other, waiting for a calm that never came, hoping for a short break and just a moment of calm water and the dimple of a rise. Maybe, he thought, the water would calm in a few minutes, when the distant clouds blew in and the weather changed a bit, or when the sun finally set, and the breezes normally lay down, when the last hour of light brought a stillness that always lasted throughout the night. The wind continued to blow; however, even at night while in bed, he would hear it rattle the windows and doors of the old house and make the fence outside sway and creak against the gusts. He would awaken in the morning to the same sounds of its whistling and roaring as it kicked up dust across the parking lot, with the tumbleweeds rolling across the highway and lodging in the chain link fence, dust devils whirling the sand and scraps of paper, creating holocaust-like tornados for the ants that happened to venture into its path. All day long the wind blew and blew, wearing down even the innermost parts of his resolute constitution for fishing. This wind had worn him down thin and if it could reach him there; where nothing else could reach, it was treading into dangerous territory. The last thing Jay needed was for something like this to find a chink in his armor; already on edge from the months of insomnia he had been battling. He was afraid that time away from the water could send him reeling over a precipice. His fishing and this river were his last bastions of sanity and where he drew his strength and there was no way he could afford to have that taken from him now. If there was anything else more important in his life than the peace that fishing brought him, he sure as hell didn't know what it was.

The wind continued every day, days when there was nothing but clear blue New Mexico sky, days when the sky was overcast and cloudy, and days when the wind would drive the cold rain sideways. The gusts made the river look more like the ocean, with breaking whitecaps sending a spray off the water, leaving him reeling like a drunkard sideways against it. He both silently prayed and cursed it to stop. Then finally having enough of it all, he would retreat to the willows, where he could lie on his back creating a break, staring up at the big cumulus clouds. As they rolled by, the clouds, themselves, saw no respite from the wind's relentlessness. He would watch the swallows, their small aerodynamic bodies seemingly oblivious to the wind's effects, until an occasional gust would send them hurtling past in a green iridescent blur that reminded him of a kaleidoscope. Abruptly, the small birds would turn on a dime and regroup, fluttering and skimming the water's surface for insects small enough to seem invisible. Frustration racked his brain in knowing that there were plenty of bugs out there and that if this wind would just stop, the fish would rise, and fishing that was now barely tolerable, would instantly become fantastic. The hopeless, powerless feeling to do anything to overcome this element of nature gripped Jay's brain like a vise. He could handle the snow, rain, or extreme cold, but this, this wind, was something he just could not bear. He became so consumed with this constant bluster, that when he wasn't watching its rippled effects upon the water, he was constantly looking for signs of its demise in the big American flag at the post office that he could see from the window of his house, or in the cheatgrass on the side of the highway on his way to the water, or in the sway of the big cottonwoods that stood in the distance off the banks of the river. Every blade of grass, creosote bush, or willow became his barometer. He watched them all like a hawk, his eyes constantly drawn toward them, waiting for that one moment when they would not move at all, signaling that it had finally stopped.

The caliche dust that was borne on the wind dropped into canyons just as it had for millenniums past, with all things changing through time, but this; of all things, remained constant- the wind and its effects. The valley filled with a brown cloud from the unabated wind, blotting out the spring sunshine that normally bathed "the small drinking town with a fishing problem", as the t-shirt said. It was the only place he knew, where the local post office, posted a sign on the front door that said "No Cleats", and the counter displayed a TU sticker. This was a town where Jay and most others were drawn merely for its piscatorial pleasures and raw natural beauty, sprinkled with a few folks that had been just born into it and never left, mostly the former. The majority of them seemed to be running from or to something they were always at a loss to describe to others; or if they even knew, were reluctant to reveal. Everyone in the local store discussed the wind situation each day, whether a fishermen, rancher, oilfield worker, or housewife, all were affected in some way or the other, and not a single one of them liked or cared for this unsettling wind. So, despite all of his studying of the weather reports and monitoring the position of the jet stream, and all his sanguine expectations, the wind just kept on doing as it wished, leaving him to deal with its consequences.

He dealt with it as best as he could, trying not to let this get down into that new place he had created for himself, the place that was free of most of the worries that had troubled him so, worries that now seemed so ephemeral. Moving out here into the open had changed him and his tastes were also simpler now. Oh, he had chased a few women in his time and had a few that had chased him as well-- albeit; one was around the table with a butcher knife. But, the so called "lusts of the flesh" did not dominate his thoughts near as much anymore, whether given way to age, or complacency, he couldn't quite discern, but he was more or less ambivalent about it and; for the most part, he welcomed the freedom from the fetters such relationships sometimes bore. Either way, the town here didn't offer much for those types of opportunities and he had managed to fill most of that in with the simple pursuit of just chasing fish. That so far, suited him just fine. He figured that if he could just reach old age without too much pain and suffering and have a pair of waders that didn't leak, he would chalk the whole thing up as a big success. So; for now, he was content to have his life "measured out in those coffee spoons" and allowed himself the luxury of going a little longer between haircuts, not shaving every day, and letting his truck go a little longer between washes.

Still there was this wind, and despite what the good book said: "That the wind goeth toward the south, and turneth about to the north; it whirleth about continually and the wind returneth again according to his circuits", Jay couldn't diminish his angst for it any less. This overpowering feeling of helplessness against an invisible enemy only seemed to make him more determined to find a way to overcome it. Giving up and giving in just wasn't in his nature when it came to fishing, but he was beginning to wonder if his "stick to your guns" policy, rather than adopt and adjust, was being carried just a little too far in this case. Now this policy of – dry flies or be damned- with this present, incessant howling, whirling, and whooshing, be damned, it seemed to be. He remembered reading about Lee Wulff's obsession with catching an Atlantic Salmon on a size 26 dry fly and his many fishless days in that pursuit, and he totally grasped the concept of that challenge, both of them knowing that there were easier ways to get the job done with better results, but none quite so rewarding. The contest had now turned from simply man versus fish to man versus fish under extremely difficult conditions, and he wanted desperately to prevail. This aberrant wind with its deleterious effects, left him hollowed out, dumbfounded, feeling this was his albatross and his cross to bear.

As if the physical effects of this Mexican originated sirocco were not enough, the nonstop cacophony of its din and bluster seemed only to make more difficult any type of concentration for rational thought, such as to how to overcome it. And still it came, deep across the sandy flat plains of the Mexican desert, into the badlands of Arizona, where the cacti and palo verde offered little defense, across the sage covered low country of New Mexico, driving with it the sand and the dust, forcing rattlesnakes, jackrabbits, coyotes, and mule deer down into the arroyos or deeper into the canyons for a safe harbor against its effects. Now, the wind was here, funneled into some preternatural vortex as it pushed its way up the river valley surrounded on both sides by the high sandstone buttes, and finding him on a personal level, waging his Quixotic battle with it there, his 4 wt. Sage rod fashioning as his lance.

Wading knee deep, Jay put the wind to his back and began pushing toward the big island not far to his right, all the time eyeing the slough approximately 40 yards away, near its middle. That slough just might offer enough protection with its surrounding willows and tamarisk to get a cast off, and he had seen fish holding in there a few times before. Making his way up the edge of the island he thought he saw a slight movement in the water, just at the corner where the slough emptied into the main channel of the river. He immediately froze in his tracks, focusing on the spot, and a few seconds later, he was able to make out the faintest outline of a rising fish.

Near the corner, very tight against the bank, he saw a rather large tuft of grass, still brown from the winter, which hung slightly down into the slow moving water. A number of midges were beginning to hatch along the bank of the island, and as they floated out of the slough they began to be carried into the main current, where they temporarily gathered in clusters behind the slack water created from the overhanging grass. Occasionally, a group would break loose with the current and the head of a very large rainbow would rise, rhythmically, like the breaching of a submarine, inhale, and slowly disappear back into the calmer water near the bank. He stood for what seemed a long time, watching that large head appear and vanish, then suddenly realizing that he was holding his breath; he relaxed and exhaled. The wind gusted at his back and whipped his wading jacket like a flag in a gale, staggering him a step forward and forcing him to readjust his footing to brace himself against it. He studied the distance and the angle between himself and the fish, guessing that he was now about 30 feet or so from where it was holding, a very doable cast in normal conditions, but with this wind there was a chance that something could, and would go wrong, most likely the line and leader being driven down onto the water with a splash, spooking the fish. He would have to get a little closer and would need to increase his angle a little more to the left; in order to keep his leader above and to the side, out of the fish's field of vision. He quickly surveyed the situation again and picked out the spot that he would need to move to in order to make his best presentation. Cautiously, he began to move slightly to his left and up, making sure not to create a wake with his movement. The fish was still rising and feeding in his slow rhythmic pattern, and he knew this was to his advantage, because the trout's guard would be down a bit while his focus was on the plentiful supply of food, constantly drifting before him. The trick would be to get just close enough to pull this off, but not too close to spook the feeding fish before the chance passed to float a fly past the nose of the trout.

As he moved upward, Jay suddenly felt and knew when he had reached the right position. He checked the condition of his fly and realized that the midge imitation he had on would be much too small to match the clusters that were being targeted by this fish. Taking every precaution to make all his movements as slow and deliberate as possible, he kept the rod tip pointed away from the fish, while he slowly clipped the fly from his line and replaced it with a newer, bigger, size 20 Griffith's Gnat. The wind continued to blow and gust, making the tying process harder, and he tried to focus on the task at hand, all the while keeping his peripheral vision glued to that reappearing head, now 20 feet above and to his right. When he had finally cinched down the knot, he clipped the tag end of the light tippet, and let out a long sigh. Relaxing, he waited for as much of a break in the wind as he could expect, and made one false cast directly to his front to measure the distance, keeping the line and the leader well to the left of the fish. It looked just about right, and on the next delivery, he threw in a little turn to the right and let the tip of the rod drop just a bit and the line slid effortlessly through the guides. The fly and leader floated toward the water as soft as a pair of thin silk panties gliding over soft, velvety knees and drifting toward the floor. At this stage in his life, either image evoked about the same level of excitement, and both seemed to have about the same effect upon him.

The instant the fly touched the water, he could tell that the drift would not be effective. The distance was perfect, but in an effort to make a soft presentation, he had pulled his punch just a little too much at the end of the cast, and the fly had fallen about 8 inches or so to the left of the fish's feeding lane. He allowed the fly to drift well past the target before picking up his line, in order not to spook the fish. Raising the rod tip, the leader and fly swung back into his free hand, just before another gust nearly sent him reeling. He recalculated and picked a spot just behind where the grass touched the water, but tighter to the bank than where all the clusters were forming, maybe an inch or two from the actual edge of the island. That would have to be where the fly needed to land, in an area about the size of a silver dollar. Too far toward the bank, and the fly wouldn't catch the current, too far forward and it would likely get caught in the clump of overhanging grass, too far back would put it too close to the fish and cause him to spook. There was only a slim chance he could pull it off, especially in this wind, but he knew he had to give it a try.

Once more he waited as another gust from the wind rocked him and nearly blew his cap off. The second it died down he let go with another cast, accentuated with a little grunt at the end to put the fly that extra few inches towards the target. The fly landed just where he had wanted it, and the big head appeared a foot downstream and slowly sipped in another cluster of naturals, while his fly held motionless in the slack water behind the grass. He held his breath as the current slowly surrounded the fly and began to pull it into the path with the remaining clusters. In a split second it began to move and soon melted and disappeared, indiscernible from all the others, as it made its way towards the ring of the fish's last rise. He lowered his profile and squinted his eyes in an effort to better distinguish his fly from the other midge clusters, but it was no use. If the fish rose, he would have to trust his instinct on whether to set the hook or not, relying on his experience to calculate the time and distance of the drift to determine if the fly would be in the proper position for the take. He'd done it hundreds of times before, but somehow this time mattered more than all of those.

Involuntarily, he held his breath again, muscles tense, and eyes strained to the spot where he had last seen the fish. Then there it was, that same giant head appearing in the slow, rhythmic manner as before, not the violent, slashy, rise of a small fish, but a nonchalant appearance, more so than a rise— deliberate, confident, and fearless, as only a big fish will do. A nanosecond passed and brain and synapses fired in unison, his heart stopped in his chest and the earth stopped turning for that moment, that one brief moment as the head disappeared and his rod tip lifted at just the right speed, at just the right moment and as his line hand made a downward movement, he felt the weight of the fish. At exactly that moment, this fish, this majestic rainbow, felt the sting of something foreign and thousands of years of genetics came together, triggering his mechanism for an instinct of flight, but the tension of rod, line, and leader, along with his sudden burst of movement, served only to roll him onto his back in a less defensible position.

Line tight, with the flexible tip of the rod bowing and flawlessly doing its work while the fly line was stripped through the guides, the fish remained off balance, unable to use his size, speed, or weight to their full advantage. There was a distinct need for expediency here in not allowing this fish to right himself and head to open water where the conditions favored the fish. This had to end this while the odds were still in the favor of the fisherman. Like a boxer reeling from a devastating blow, the fish gave it his all, fighting from his disadvantageous position with a series of shakes and lunges, but the tension of the line and pressure from the rod prevented him from ever righting himself into proper fighting position. With the fly line trapped against the butt of the rod in one hand he deftly slid the other hand with the net under the back of the fish and felt the muscles of his forearm strain against the full weight and heft of this magnificent creature. He took a deep breath and looked at the fish as the cold, clear water ran over it in the net. Still fresh from the short fight, the gill plates of the trout slowly pulsated and the big rainbow seemed to still resonate that same feeling of confidence he had shown as he fed, with no look of fear in his eyes. Firm, strong, muscular flesh armored with bright, silvery skin, accentuated with slight pinkish broad stripes and an impressive girth, he lay there unmoving while the tiny hook was removed and the net was lowered. He righted himself facing upstream, exposing a broad dark green back, speckled with tiny, jet black dots. As he took his buoyancy and the net drifted down to a right angle, he pushed away with a regal air, showing no certain concern for the need of neither speed nor safety, just a slow melting away in a forward motion to invisibility.

Jay looked at the darkening sky, feeling the slack of his muscles as the tension dissipated from his body. For the first time since this all began he realized that the wind was still blowing hard. Placing the bend of the hook through the keeper on the rod, he reeled up the slack line until he felt it tighten on the reel. He looked around, marveling at the beauty of this place and thought of the beauty and pureness of this experience. As he turned he noticed the grey stolid appearance the water had taken on from the oncoming darkness and suddenly felt the coldness of the wind on his face as he looked downriver and headed to the parking lot where he knew his would be the only car there at this late hour, just as it always was. Later that night, he awakened, and as he lay there in the stillness of a darkened room, he realized the wind had stopped. A slight smile began at the corners of his mouth and slowly spread, deepening across the rest of his face as he felt himself drifting, disappearing, back into sleep, back into invisibility.

3/4/2012

Oh boy, oh boy, oh boy! After weeks of suffering through adverse weather conditions on Mondays and Tuesdays, I'm about to catch a break and have some of the best weather early March can offer here, and the rest of the week looks nice, as well. The way I see it is that I've paid my dues, and mid to high 50's with lots of sunshine will be my just reward for suffering through on those days when conditions were more conducive to sitting indoors by the fire, sorting my fly boxes and cleaning my fly lines, than standing in the river waving a stick. Even with the less than favorable conditions this past week, the fishing was still good and if you're one of the lucky ones that will be arriving here this week; well, you've got that to look forward to, plus the bonus of nicer climatic conditions. As far as effective fishing goes, it's still mostly small midge patterns like size 24 and 26 Krystal Flash in grey and black, and the obligatory Red Larva in size 18; as well as, those assorted pupae patterns, such as Abe's Silk Midge and UFO's. If you are one of those guys or gals that prefer to take your fish with dry fly patterns, there will still be plenty of opportunities to do just that with small midge patterns between the hours of 10:00 a.m. and 3:00 p.m., so don't fret about being left out, if that's your thing. I prefer the Fore and Aft pattern in size 24 in such circumstances, fished on 7x fluorocarbon. I know there some out there that may doubt the need for the fluorocarbon bit, and there are skeptics that say that it may actually be more visible to fish than mono in such circumstances, but from my experience, that just ain't so. In the worst case scenario, I view it like chicken soup for a cold--"it may not really cure anything, but it sure isn't gonna hurt anything, either." Something I might offer to those that are new to fishing dries to San Juan fish, try a slightly downstream and across presentation. I like to pick out an individual rising fish and position myself across and slightly above the target, cast about 2 to 3 feet above and beyond the rise, then drag the fly back and towards you until it is in the fish's feeding lane, and drop the rod tip allowing the fly enough slack to drift right over the nose of the fish. You'll find that the initial movement of the fly will cause your eyes to key in on its location and you'll be able to see it a lot better, than when you just randomly chuck it out there and hope for the best. There's a reason why they call that "blind casting." Dropping the rod tip will also allow the fly to be presented in a drag free manner with less slack line to recover on a rising fish. Sometimes it's difficult to see the fly, or you may lose it from your field of vision on the drift, but with enough practice you'll learn to know where it "should" be, and if you see a rise, go ahead and set the hook--all you are out is a cast, and you can always pick up and try again. With the bright sunshine we are expecting, I don't really know what to expect in the way of the baetis hatches we have been experiencing lately, I guess we'll just have to wait and see, although I have seen some pretty good hatches on those bluebird sky days, as well. If it does happen it will most likely take place between 1:00 and 3:00 from the Baetis Bend down to Pump House Run area. I would carry some CDC RS2s, Grey and Chocolate Foam Wings, Rootbeer patterns; as well as, some Comparadun patterns, in my box if I fished any of those areas. If you would like to book a guide trip, or need more info give us a call at 505-632-2194. I would like to also mention that there will be a volunteer project going on this Saturday in the Braids location beginning at 10:00 a.m., which will entail reseeding the new improvement areas with grass, to allow for the mitigation of erosion to the recent work there, during the upcoming release of high flows this spring. If you can donate a few hours of your time, the affair is "BYOR"- Bring You Own Rake- and the help will be greatly appreciated.

3/11/2012

I'll be the first to admit that I am a wimp when it comes to dealing with not feeling well. So, I'll apologize in advance for the lack of extemporaneous superfluousness, usually associated with this article. No doubt, many will be pleased that the power of the common cold has dictated the brevity of this report and for once they can get the updated skinny on San Juan fishing without plodding through a lot of extra verbiage and side stories of my past fishing exploits. We've got some great weather headed our way this week, with some expected temperatures in the 60's. It doesn't look like the wind that we saw today will be around for most of the week, so that is an added bonus. The flow is just under 500 cfs and the water visibility is still around 2 and a half to 3 feet. There's still some good midge hatches coming off from around 10:00 till 3:00, especially in the upper river. Small midge patterns--size 24 to 26, in black and grey will get the job done when there aren't a lot of risers, and adult midge dries in the same size, when you start to see heads. Red larvas from size 18 to 24 are still working well, especially during the morning hours. The streamer fishing is still good with white and olive bunny leeches, still producing. From Baetis Bend and below we're still seeing a good BWO hatch, that is starting around 1:30 and lasting some days until well after 3:00. It's not a blanket hatch, but it's enough to get a lot of good fish up and seems to actually fish better than those heavy hatch days when your fly is competing with too many naturals on the water. I really like the CDC Comparadun pattern in size 22 for this action, and any number of baetis nymphs such as, Fluff Baetis, RS2s, and Foamwings in grey and chocolate are great for the shoulders of the hatch. Well, there you have it--I'll now relegate myself back to the couch with my bottle of Nyquil, in hopes that I will have improved my condition enough by tomorrow, to get back out on the water.

3/18/2012

March Madness! I love watching college basketball this time of year. These young players pour their heart and soul into their play and put everything they've got on the line to win. Sure there's talent in the NBA playoffs, but I'll bet you (or Mitt Romney), $10,000 that you'll never see those NBA guys crying on camera, in the locker room after a loss. We've got our own form of March Madness going on right here at the San Juan. Lots of Spring Breakers and Weekend Warriors, suiting up and double checking their equipment in the parking lots and putting all they've got into the preparation for battle with their adversaries of elusive rainbow and brown trout. They're going to have to battle some pretty oppugnant conditions for the next few days, high winds on Sunday, Winter on Monday (with rain and snow), then a 20 degree drop in temperatures from our past 60 plus highs, on Tuesday. It's what people, who live here, call "typical Spring weather", it'll be back to nearly 70 degrees on Wednesday and the rest of the week. We still have wintertime flows, just under 500 cfs (spring releases probably won't start until sometime near the end of May) and water visibility near two and a half to three feet. There's decent midge hatches on most days between 10:00 a.m. till 300 p.m. and you can fool a good number of fish on red larva and assorted small midge patterns if you're into nymph fishing. You'll also have the opportunity to catch some fish on small midge dry patterns; throughout most of the day, you'll just have to move around a little to find the risers. In the areas from Baetis Bend and lower, it's a mix of midges and baetis patterns like RS2's, fluff baetis, rootbeers, and foamback emergers. There has also been enough of a hatch of BWO's in this area; between 1:30 till 3:00, to get the fish looking up, and BWO patterns in the dry variety can get you into fish. Streamer fishing will probably get you into some bigger fish, but don't look for the numbers that nymphing or dry fly fishing are more likely to produce. Overall, the fishing has been good here for weeks, but with the change in the weather and the adverse conditions it will bring, that Cinderella Story that we're all looking for is more likely to take place from Wednesday until the end of the week.

3/26/2012

I've been to a lot of fly shops from Alaska and British Columbia to all up and down the East Coast, to pretty much everywhere out West, and I've talked to countless others on the phone, and I'll have to say that the information I've received about their home rivers has run the gamut from invaluable to useless, and even sometimes possibly deceptive, bordering on outright lies. On the Big Hole River in Montana, one guy told me exactly where to park and what path to take, that ended at the edge of a small feeder channel that held some big fish, right where he said they'd be, so uncanny that I think the only things he left out were the names he's probably given to each of those fish. Another time I was planning a trip to a place in Colorado but it was borderline on runoff time, so I made a call there to make sure that the river wasn't blown out before I drove all the way across the entire state. I was told it was "just a little off color, with good visibility along the edges--still fishing good." I arrived later that day to a river out of its banks and the color and consistency of chocolate milk; and given the weather, I'm sure that it didn't just happen over the last few hours. Anyway, the point I'm trying to make here is that there are some places where you can take what they tell you as the gospel, and there are others where you're better off getting a second opinion. I'm going to have to take a few weeks away from this column, for medical reasons, so if you rely on this report for your San Juan fishing information, you're going to have to call the shop to find out what's going on. Don't worry; I'm leaving you in good hands. All those guys there fish the river a lot and they know their stuff; and moreover, they're honest. As far as this week goes, the river is fishing great, and the weather is going to be warm and sunny. Nymphing with small midge patterns has been productive, although your best results are going to probably come from size 26 patterns in black. UV midges, Crystal Flash, and Bling midges, seem to be the ticket. The flow is just under 500 cfs and the water clarity is good and you can still find plenty of rising fish between 10:00 am, and 3:00 p.m., if you like fishing small midge dry patterns. We're still seeing decent BWO hatches, but they seem to be located from the Simon Canyon area and below. The timing for these hatches has been a little tricky lately, with reports of them coming off some days as early as 11:30 and as late as 2:00 on others, so you'll just have to play that one by ear and be ready with some olive Comparaduns, if you plan on catching that hatch. One thing is for sure, you can't beat the weather we're having right now, so if you decide to come bring your sunscreen. We really haven't seen the high winds yet; that usually start around this time of year, and the weather report for this week is not showing them in the upcoming forecast. It's been a strange year for weather, so who knows what will happen with that, later this spring. With the warmer temperatures, it's a good time to fish the more predictable flows of tailwaters, or you could always make a call to some shop on a freestone somewhere and roll the dice like I did, that time I drove across the bigger part of the great state of Colorado, at least the scenery is nice this time of year.

5/6/2012

For those of you that follow this report, you know that I've been out of commission for about a month due to health issues. To borrow a few lines from Willie Nelson: "It's been rough and rocky travelin', but I'm finally standing upright on the ground." I'm happy to report that I am now back to work, and most of all I'm fishing again, which I consider an essential part of the healing process, or what I like to call "chicken soup for the soul." We've really been blessed with a beautiful Spring; with great weather and great fishing conditions, warm sunshine and not so much of the wind that we normally see at this time of the year. I can't remember when we've had such wonderful weather start so early in the year and continue unabated all throughout the season. Just more reasons to get out and fish, if you really need more reasons. This next week will be your big chance to get in your last hurrah on the Juan, before the spring water releases start on the 13th. Weather-wise, you can expect some cooler temperatures; especially in the earlier part of the week, with a chance of some thundershowers, but the good news here looks like we will see some good cloud cover that could bring on some good BWO hatches, and the wind looks like it might cooperate to allow for some good dry fly fishing Comparadun patterns, especially in the lower river. There was some baetis activity in that area last week, but the hatch was quite sparse and most of the fish that were looking up, were keying in on midge patterns. Something to note; however, is that a lot of the Baetis we were seeing, were duns with mahogany bodies, so I would plan accordingly for this upcoming week. On the rest of the river, we've seen some really good midge hatches that start to get into full swing around 11:00 and last throughout most of the day, with lots of fish rising to the Fore and Aft pattern, if you are into fishing dry patterns. I'm having best results using 7 x tippets on these size 24 patterns, but if it's a bit windy with a light chop on the water you can get by with 6x. During the shoulder times, when you see all those fish porpoising, Chocolate Foam Wings, fished shallow and in the film, have been real producers. Team up that foam wing with a midge emerger pattern and I think you are going to be in for some great fishing this week. If the wind does come up, I know a lot of people like to switch over to nymph rigs, to avoid going cross-eyed, trying to follow those small dry patterns on the water, but I've found some willing fish on size 16 foam ant patterns during this time, especially if the fish are actively feeding in the upper water column. You won't have every fish you cast to take that pattern, but you'll find enough to keep you busy, especially if you concentrate on those fish holding in the faster water around 1 and 1/2 to 2 feet deep and along the edges. For those die-hards that like to stay out there late, I've had some real fine fishing from 6:00 pm, right up till dark on a late midge hatch, especially if the wind stays down, so if you want to stretch out your fishing day, it's a time I would not overlook. If you're planning a trip after this week, my experience has been that the conditions during the period when the water is rising (13th through the 16th) can be a little tough, with the fish moving around a lot to adjust to changing currents and increased turbidity in the water. A day or so after the water has been at 5,000 cfs, the fishing can be good, but it's best fished (and safest), from a boat. The last few days (24th and 25th) can be downright fantastic, and you can find large numbers of big fish that are healthy, hungry, and easy to spot in the clear water, against a scoured clean river bottom. So there you have it, plenty of good reasons to get out and make the most of it this week.

5/13/2012

An endless sky that seems to go on forever, so preternatural blue that you would swear sometimes it was painted on the roof of the world. Countless green junipers, hanging on brown sandstone walls, in sweeping desert vistas. A pace of life that turns a bit slower, here in the Land Of Enchantment. I can't see how you could come up with a better backdrop for world-class fly fishing by man-made design. Sure, you don't always have the luxury of a Starbucks on every corner, the electric power grid sometimes rivals that of a third world country, and out here your Smartphone won't seem quite so smart in a lot of spots, and even that man made convenience called the internet can take on a deliberate lack of verisimilitude at times. All a small price to pay in my book, for the blessing of living in trout Nirvana. There are trade-offs down every path of this thing we call life. Pick your poisons carefully. This coming week, it would appear that those of us that will have the good fortune to be on the water here will have benefitted from a temporary stay of execution; if you will, from the Bureau Of Reclamation. The spring high flow releases have tentatively been moved back until May 21st, barring any more last minute changes, all this will apparently be solidified by a final decision by 5:00 p.m. on Monday the 14th, or so we're told. For those of you that live out of the area and have been trying to make plans to visit, I know these changes have been creating some logistical nightmares, but hang in there; we should have some definitive information soon. If you are lucky enough to be out this week, expect the continuation of some great fishing and more good weather. There have been some really good midge hatches, that are starting a little later in the day (12:00 or so) and a good mix of BWOs that get going around 1:00 and lasting up until 3:00. I had some fantastic dry fly fishing in the middle flats last week on a size 22 comparadun pattern, and I saw more BWOs up there than I have seen in a very long time, the bugs were actually quite larger than my size 22, but those were the largest in my box at the time. They worked fine, but it sure would have been nice to fish something bigger, for the sake of my eyesight. For nymphing it's been the usual suspects, with Chocolate Foam Wings, producing almost anywhere in the river. Small midge pupae and emerger patterns in grey, olive and black are still good choices when the fish are subsurface and larger midge patterns like Tav's Big Mac and Abe's Midge Master are working well in the upper flats to the Cable Hole. Of course, there's the good ol' Fore and Aft for those fish rising to midge adults and CDC Comparaduns, when you start seeing baetis. Hopefully, you'll have been blessed by luck or happenstance to end up here this week and enjoy the windfall of the decision to move the water release dates back; if not, give us a call after Monday and we can let you know when to book your next trip. After this short window of high water it looks like we have a lot of summer left for some more great fishing on the Juan.

5/20/2012

Into every life a little rain must fall. After months of great fishing and stable water conditions, things are about to change here on the San Juan. Tonight while most of us are asleep the BOR will begin releasing around 2,000 cfs of water, now held back from the earthen impoundment we know as Navajo Dam and continue to ramp it up until it reaches 5,000 cfs on Wednesday. This will all be part of a 7 day flush at 5,000 cfs which will taper down over a 2 day period and return to the 500 cfs level, by June 1st. It's something that happens every year; and no doubt, a necessary evil, but that doesn't seem to make it any easier to bear, for those of us that like to fish here. I guess the good news is that it will all be over relatively soon, compared to the prolonged schedules I have seen in some years past, and it really does a nice job of cleaning up the river bottom of lots of debris and unwanted didymo. Afterwards, I think it fishes better, but maybe those are just my feelings from pent up demand, caused from being off the water for a week. I do know that the sight fishing part of it is better, the fish are a lot easier to see against a clean bottom and the clarity of the water gets a lot better than before the release. The first few days after the release starts can create some tough fishing, there's a lot of stuff coming down, and the fish are moving around a lot and seem a little confused. After a few days at 5,000 cfs, things start to mellow out a bit and the fish start to stack up in their new lies and adjust, the water clears and the fish are pretty easy to find, stacked up in runs out of the main current, they are safer and more easily reached from a boat during this time, and the fishing can be very good. If you're out there on the first few days, your best bet is to throw some big, bright stuff. This is the time for San Juan Worms, brightly colored Egg patterns, big Sparkle worms, Red Larva, Annelids and Streamers in white, black, and olive. Of course you'll have to chunk on a lot more weight than you are accustomed to fishing at 500 cfs. On the last few days as the water drops, you can find some big pods of fish stacked up in a lot of places, and this can produce some good fishing. You'll just have to use some caution and good old common sense about where you can and can't wade, but I generally find a lot of healthy and hungry fish during this time. It's all part of a cycle we've grown somewhat accustomed to over the years, and compared to some freestone rivers that occasionally remain unfishable for time measured in months, I guess it's a small price to pay.

5/22/2011

Hopefully this past week was the last week of the crazy spring weather we have been experiencing for the past few months. The cooler temperatures and precipitation in the form of snow that hit the San Juans on our northern border, stalled out the Animas runoff, and resulted in the delay of increased spring releases from Navajo Dam, as noted in the update listed below. For those of you that cancelled plans for the Memorial Day week and weekend, you can now reformulate and plan on some warm weather, lower flows, and great fishing. Monday's high will be around 70 and Tuesday looks to be a bit cooler with a high of only 64, but the rest of the week will start to warm with highs reaching into the 80's. We had some good solid fishing this past week with some great midge hatches that lasted throughout most of the day; however, the baetis hatches that we had been seeing, have seemed to slow a bit, limiting the opportunity to fish blue winged olive patterns, in the dry variety. The standard process of nymphing with small dark midge patterns in the morning is still effective, and baetis patterns, such as RS2s, Fluff Baetis, and Chocolate Foam Wings are still taking lots of fish in the lower portion of the river, despite the absence of heavy hatches of adult blue winged olives. There are still ample opportunities to fish small midge dry patterns throughout most of the day, especially with great water clarity and flows around 500cfs, which allow for some great sight fishing. Overall, it looks like this week you can put away the gloves and wool caps and break out the sunscreen and enjoy a reprieve from the planned, earlier release schedule for a few weeks more, and spend some quality time on the water.

5/27/2012

I'm going to go ahead and show my age here and use the lyrics from a Tom Petty song to describe my feelings about the fishing on the San Juan right now, and say that "The waiting is the hardest part." Or maybe I should exercise my poetic license and change that to, "The wading is the hardest part." Either way, if you're wondering how the fishing has been this past week, I'd describe it as a lot like Chuck Norris--tough and kinda dangerous. With present flows exceeding 5,200 cfs, the best and safest way to fish it is from a boat, and with someone that is very experienced with this water, at the oars. Anything else, you're risking life and limb for a chance to hook a trout, and that's just a little too risky in my book, and I'm an extremist when it comes to challenging the conditions, for a chance to fish. Throw in those 50 mile per hour wind gusts we saw this Saturday that turned the landscape here into something reminiscent to the Dust Bowl, and you've got yourself a real challenge. But with the wind dying down for the next week, and the water clearing, and the fish settling into their new holding patterns, you can have some very productive days on the water, provided you do it in the prescribed fashion from the safety of a boat, with an experienced guide and required safety-flotation devices. If you're out there, concentrate on the first 10 feet from the bank; out of the main current, and rig with the high water selections like bright egg patterns, sparkle worms, san juan worms, big annelid patterns, and streamers, using one BB shot in most places, and two number six weights in the back eddies and side channels when you're out of the current. Move the indicator up to about six feet or so, and you should get into fish. If you're planning on wading, I think it's best to wait until at least Wednesday, when the water will drop to 3,400 cfs; or better yet Thursday, when it reaches 2,200 cfs, to do your fishing. Just remember to still exercise caution at those levels, especially if you're not experienced with this river. The fishing can be great during this time when the water levels are dropping and after it returns back to 500 cfs, on Friday. To me it's worth the wait, the water will be crystal clear, the river bottom is scoured clean from all the moss and didymo and the fish are easier to spot. In the meantime, I'm going to spend the next few days targeting some smallmouth on the lake, with the fly rod. Yeah, the waiting is hard, but we've got a lot of summer still ahead of us, and believe me it will be worth it.

5/29/2011

This past week produced some nicer spring- like weather than what we have been seeing for the past few months and some more pleasant fishing conditions, with the exception of some real windy conditions on Saturday and Sunday. This next week will start out with a much cooler Monday, with the high reaching into only the low 60s, but then will bounce right back into the low 80s on Tuesday and stay in that range through the week. There will be some breezy days, and a chance of thundershowers on Wednesday and Thursday, but no call for those real windy, gusty days that will challenge and frustrate even the best of fly fishermen. This will be the last week of flows in the 500 cfs range, as Monday, June 6th marks the ramp up towards the high water release (see details below). The methods for fooling these San Juan fish will remain pretty much the same this week, as they have for the past few. Nymphing with small dark midge patterns (Crystal Flash, Black Beauties, Jujube, etc.) in sizes 24 and smaller will be consistent throughout the day. I would also mix this up with larger midge patterns such as Tav's Big Mac and Abe's Midgemaster as one of my flies, as there have been good reports on both working in areas from the Texas Hole and higher up the river. Below Texas Hole, RS2s, Rootbeers, and Small Flashback Pheasant Tails are still producing fish, despite the fact there has been a significant decrease in the Blue Wing Olive hatch, we had been seeing in weeks past. It's important to remember that the San Juan is; and will always be, a very technical river, so drag free drifts and presentations are key, if you want to get into fish. Be prepared to fish 6x tippets and small weights, and adjust your strike indicator to get your flies into the level of the water column where the fish are feeding. There are also ample opportunities to fish some dry flies right now, but you will need to be alert and opportunistic, and be able to read the hatch and how the fish are reacting to it. One thing is a given on this, it is most likely to be rises to midges right now, and the patterns that will be most effective are gonna be small midge imitations (Fore and Afts, Griffith's Gnats, Black Midge Adults) in sizes 24 and smaller. All this being said, there are still some big smart fish out there that sometimes do dumb things, and I have had lots of fun the past few weeks fishing some larger terrestrial patterns to these rising fish, so don't be afraid to throw some big foam ants and beetles at those fish you see rising to those tiny black midges. The guys at our shop spend a lot of time on this water and know many of its idiosyncrasies well, so don't hesitate to call or stop in for advice, they'll be happy to share their knowledge. Our guides have been fishing this river for a lot of years; as well, and can really cut down your learning curve and get you into fish a lot sooner than trying to figure all this out on your own, through trial and error, so give us a call.

Summer

Jay Walden

2 SUMMER

Almost September

The days warm more slowly now
The summer sun not so intense

The grasshoppers rise later now
Waiting for that warm glow
In the shadowgrass along the fence

Late evening smells of rain, creosote, and sage
And the smell of roasted chiles and ripe peaches

As earlier shadows grow
Creeping toward their far reaches

It'll rain soon, turn cold
And won't warm again till spring

Long endless days
Filled with cold and dark
Winter; seems now,
Like not such a distant thing

And I'll long for and miss these days,
When it's almost September.

6/3/2012

Well, it's happening. I'm headed down the road to "Geezerdom." Old Fart City here I come. While being vicissitudinous has never been one of my stronger suites, lately I see the formation of habit and routine creeping more and more into my daily life as I grow a little older and nowhere is it more prevalent these days than in my fishing. The way I see it, I'm just a few steps away from that guy that strikes terror into the hearts of young children that have to enter my yard to retrieve their lost ball. It's what my hillbilly relatives back in the Appalachian Mountains would refer to as "set in his ways." While custom and convention have their positive attributes in life (I would probably struggle with the task of making the morning coffee without them) they can limit your sense of adventure and your proclivity to try different things. Young people beware. However; I guess one of the benefits of spending your fair share of time on this old planet is that you have the time to discover what you really like and hopefully get pretty good at it, or it's that one of the joys of growing older and becoming a curmudgeon is that you can do as you damn well please. Anyway, it seems that as I advance in age my penchant to fish dry flies, and forsake it for all the other multifarious ways of taking fish, becomes more second nature every time I go out on the water. Add to that; that as of yesterday, the water on the San Juan River just dropped to around 500 cfs and the river is in such great shape and the fish are hungry and healthy, I'm doomed. Right now begins the season to work these fish with some larger terrestrial patterns—foam ants, beetles, hoppers—flies you can actually see! The picky ones can still be taken on small midge adult patterns in grey and black—the Fore and Aft being my favorite, in size 24. If nymphing is your thing, that's hot right now too. The standard small midge patterns in assorted colors, with a focus right now on midge pupae patterns like the UFO and Bling Midge, are a good choice for the upper part of the river. As you move lower (below Texas Hole) WD-40s and Chocolate Foam Wings in size 22 and 24, should be in your offerings. The water is extremely clear and the river bottom is void of all that annoying moss and didymo, so you have the opportunity to sight fish and target some of those big fish you have been dreaming about for the last few months. It's a great time to fish the San Juan- great weather, lots of hungry fish, clear water conditions, all good things no matter what method your fishing bent is. As for me, they say it takes about 21 days of doing things differently to break a habit and I can't seem to line up that many days in a row of continuous fishing, so I guess I'll just stick to the dries for now.

6/5/2011

It looks like summer is finally here, and we had some long-awaited warm weather when the wind didn't blow all that bad, this past week. It was a good week for fishing the San Juan and lots of people seemed to take advantage of the last week of 500 cfs flows we will see for a little while. As noted below, on Monday the 6th the BOR will begin their spring release schedule with a somewhat rapid rise in water levels, until the river reaches 5,000 cfs and stays there for a week. Monday and Tuesday will still offer some tolerable water levels for those folks that are familiar with the river and know where they can and can't wade in 2,000 and 3,200 cfs conditions. The large daily increases will no doubt cause a lot of drifting debris in the water and also bring a decrease in its clarity, so be prepared to check and clean your flies, often. This will be a time to fish some larger, brighter patterns, like eggs, San Juan worms, leeches and woolly buggers. Unless you are very experienced with fishing the river at 5,000 cfs, and know where you can safely access some back channel spots, I would not recommend taking the risk and venturing into some dangerous situations that could put you into jeopardy. If you have access to a boat and someone that really knows how to navigate the river in these high water conditions, you can still get into some good fishing during the highest flows, as the fish tend to get pushed out of the main body of the current and into the slower edges and eddies in more predictable lies, so if you want to fish during Wednesday through Sunday I would recommend that you book an experienced guide. If you don't have lots of experience with these high water conditions, or access to a good experienced guide, then this may be a good week to spend some quality time at the tying table getting ready for the rest of the summer season, or getting caught up on some of those summer projects around the house, so that you can spend more time on the river, when the water starts to recede.

6/10/2012

Summertime! It's not officially here according to the calendar, but you really couldn't prove it by the weather we've been having. It's a time for barbecues, vacations, and all those other fun things we dream about out here during the winter, and most of all—long days on the water. I love the fact we get to experience all four seasons here and each one has its own merits, but summertime is my hands down favorite. Just slap on some sunscreen and bug dope, give me a bottle of water and a pocket full of dry flies and a couple of spools of tippet and I'm in heaven. I like to hit the water by 9:00 or 10:00 a.m. and if I see another car in the parking lot when I come off the river, I feel a little cheated that I didn't stay just a little longer. I just love that big blue New Mexico sky, when that hot sun seems to penetrate all the way down to my bones, while that crystal clear, icy water rushes by at my feet with big hungry trout in my crosshairs. There are times here when the fishing is good, other times when it's alright, and sometimes when it's just on fire/spectacular. Now is the time that they refer to in fly shops all across America as "You should have been here yesterday." It really is that good right now. Fishing with terrestrial patterns is my cherished way of fishing this river and it's a method that I feel is overlooked by a lot of folks that think you have to wait until all the planets align and there is that rare phenomenon called the "Ant Fall", in order to fish some flies on this river that you actually can see. I'll be the first to admit that it's probably not going to get the numbers of fish to the net you are gonna see with a standard nymph rig, but if you're throwing big foam- bodied flies to fat fish and that slow, methodical take of an ant or cartoon hopper doesn't make your heart skip a beat, then you need to stop reading this right now and call your cardiologist and get an EKG scheduled. The thing with this kind of fishing is it's a numbers game—you need to put the fly in front of as many fish as you can. If you have issues with rejection, then it's probably not going to be for you. But for me, the payoff is worth it—don't expect to catch many small fish, and fish a lighter rod, because at the end of the day you'll have cast enough times, that all the Advil in the world isn't going to help your shoulder. If you want to tilt the odds a little more in your favor, target those fish in faster water from 1 to 2 feet deep, or those hanging higher in the water column, or against the bank. For those of you that prefer other methods, the nymphing is great as well. Red larva in the morning hours and midge patterns in sizes 24 and 26's, and even 28's in olive, black, and grey, throughout the day. If you're fishing Texas Hole and below, you are going to want to throw in some Chocolate Foam Wings, RS2's and WD-40s in your repertoire. Sight fishing some conehead streamers in olive and black can be a real hoot, right now, if that's your thing. Overall, it really hard to go wrong. The fishing is great and the river is in just pristine shape. Hope you get a chance to get out this week and see what I'm so excited about and if you see that lone vehicle in the parking lot after everyone else is long gone, don't call Search and Rescue, I'll make it out eventually, I just want to make this one more cast.

6/12/2011

Hang on, just a few more days and we're there. For those of you that have been waiting out these high flows, I feel your pain. What has actually been only a few days, can sometimes feel like a lifetime, when you're waiting for the opportunity to fish. This past week was a tough one for most people that attempted to wade and fish, but the guides and the boaters were able to get into some fish, using lots of weight and some big bright colored stuff. That is pretty much gonna be the ticket until Wednesday, until the river starts to go down. By Wednesday, the river will be wade fishable in a few locations, but you'll have to be careful to pick your spots, since it will only be dropping to 3,400 cfs, by then. The fish are usually eager to come to the fly as the water drops; and you can find them in large groups during this time, but in the past the BOR has not pursued such an aggressive schedule to drop the flows; as this year, so your window of opportunity will be short for this. You'll still be able to get away with the bigger, brighter, stuff on Wednesday, using some weight to offset the current. Eggs, San Juan Worms, Sparkle Worms, Flashback Pheasant Tails and big Desert Storms work great during this time. The visibility isn't all that bad either, as most of the debris has been flushed by the 5,000 cfs release. By Thursday, the water level will have reached 2,200 cfs and opened up more of the river to wading. Red Larva in size 18 should be the ticket, and I would still try the Desert Storms, and bigger midge patterns, such as Abe's Midge Master, Tav's Big Mac, Flashback Pheasant Tails and Root Beers from the Texas Hole, on down. On Friday, we are back to 500 cfs, great weather, and the wind is even going to cooperate for a change with speeds that will only be around 13 to 15 mph, throughout the weekend. From here on it's easy sailing, using the standard nymph rigs, with small midge patterns, during most of the day, and switching to small midge dry patterns, when the opportunities present themselves. We're still several weeks away from any PMD or Caddis activity in the lower river, but we'll be keeping an eye out, and let you know when that happens.

6/17/2012

If you spend your fair share of days on the water, it's bound to happen to you. "The Black Hand", that's what one of my fishing acquaintances and a fair raconteur in his own right, Clayton Gist, calls it. Theories abound, as to its cause, ranging from lack of sleep, rushing out the door to the river without that second cup of coffee, or just simple preoccupation with the issues that surround us outside of fishing, in this thing called life. Whatever the reason, it's something you don't want to become afflicted with. It's bad "Ju-Ju", brother, and if you think that the theories for its raison d'être are myriad, there exist about as many as for the common cold, for its cure. One of the more prevalent ones is to repair oneself to the nearest bank and have a leisurely lunch, or rearrange your fly box into color-coordinated rows; or better yet, put all the flies into their order of taxonomy and zoological classification as they exist in the entomological world. Anything to restore your equanimity and as the Strother Martin Jr. character in "Cool Hand Luke" says, "get your mind right." This will also require that you count all of those fish you have been missing as "mulligans", and totally forget about them and move on. Easier said than done for me, and this past Tuesday after being just a fraction of a second too slow on too many big fish that telegraphed their take to my size 16 ant pattern in an effort to seemingly mock me, I didn't follow that advice, but went about it in my own way that LBJ referred to as "A jackass hunkering down in a hailstorm" and continued to flail away at them and curse-neither of which made the situation any better. However, later in the day I was able to get my mojo back and settled into the groove enough to get the albatross from around my neck and landed some nice fish. As for the fishing out here, it's been great since the water went back down. Still lots of action on terrestrials, even though the midge hatches are extremely sparse, and the baetis seem nonexistent; or at least so, to produce rising fish. Standard San Juan midge patterns in olive, cream, red, and black are going to work, if nymphing is your thing and I have been hearing positive things about chamois leeches, as well. The BOR increased the flow here on Saturday to around 650 cfs and I heard from several people that the fishing was a little tougher that earlier in the week, but I'm pretty confident that things will settle back quickly, an extra 150 cfs isn't such a big change, and besides I think we could use the extra water right now to open up a little more of the river and get the current moving in some of those dead still areas. Word has it that are some caddis showing up in the lower river—below the quality water line—maybe we'll see some movement this week and they'll start moving up into the Durangler's Corner/Simon Canyon area—I'll follow up on this after some more research. If you make it out this week, make sure you arrive with your game face on and don't have a morning like I did last Tuesday. Remember, it's all about the timing and you don't want your fishing partner referring to you as "Can't Get Right", from the Eddie Murphy movie "Life", as my friend does when I'm struck with a bad case of the "Black Hand."

6/19/2011

"Time is but the stream I go a-fishing in"—Henry David Thoreau. For those of you that have been waiting for the high water releases to subside, your time has now come. At present, the flow level is at 475 cfs, and looks to stay in 500 cfs range for a while. The river is in great shape right now and the high flows have scoured and cleaned the riverbed of the moss and didymo that existed earlier, resulting in gin clear conditions for fishing. Results from this past week, show the river is fishing great right now and the fish are in very good shape, with lots of reports of some big, heavy fish being caught, in all areas of the quality water section. This coming week should offer some wonderful opportunities to enjoy the San Juan, at its best. With the exception of a windy Sunday, the weather will be great; although there is a slight chance of an isolated thunderstorm on Monday, but the temperatures will be in the mid to upper 80s for the remainder of the week, with lots of clear blue New Mexico sky and sunshine. The fish will have settled back into their usual feeding lanes, that they have been accustomed to occupying during 500cfs flows, and the small midge patterns that are common to these waters, will once again become the predominate producers. The early morning hours have seen fish coming to size 18 Red

Midge Larva and Brown San Juan Worms; as well as, good reports on black streamer patterns. As the midges become more active later in the morning, Krystal Flash Midges, Black Beauties, and Mono Midges in size 26, are the go to flies. From the middle flats and below, baetis patterns, such as Fluff Baetis and Chocolate Foam Wings, have been working well. There will be opportunities to fish some dries to rising fish, so watch for those snouts on the water, once the adult bugs become numerous enough to attract the attention of the fish. I really like Fore and Afts and Tav's Griffith's Gnats, in size 24 for this type of work, and with the water clarity, you may have to go all the way down to 7x fluorocarbon tippet, to improve your chances. I have also heard good reports of large hopper patterns, taking some big fish this past week, so don't be afraid to try some bigger stuff, if you start to see some rising fish. Hope you can get out this week and enjoy this great weather and this great fishery, and it's nice to know that we probably have some of the best conditions in the west right now, with most of our neighboring waters still locked in runoff conditions.

6/24/2012

Fishing; as life itself, sometimes carries its share of little disappointments. After weeks of water conditions that produced some of the best angling so far this year on the San Juan, we were thrown one of those little curve balls that can leave you scratching your head and wondering, just where all the fish went. When you go from catching lots of fish on big foam imitations on one day, to struggling to see a fish the next, it can cause some severe psychological problems that even Dr. Phil would find hard pressed to cure. On Monday the Bureau Of Reclamation dropped the flow here from 650 cfs to 500 cfs, only to raise it again to 850 cfs on Tuesday, followed by another increase on Saturday to 1,000 cfs. If you think you're confused about what's going on, just think of how those fish out there must feel. While the result of these changes can have a temporary adverse effect on the "catching" part of the sport by moving the currents and thus the thalwegs that supply food to the fish, as well as altering the temperature of the water and affecting hatches, it may prove somewhat cathartic to the fisherman to realize that it is not some vast dark conspiracy by the BOR to just screw with your fishing. In order to gain a larger perspective of the flow change thing in the first place, it's important to note that since its inception back in 1902, the Bureau's primary purpose has been for the delivery, diversion, and storage of water for irrigation, water supply, and hydroelectric power generation, and it now provides water for over 31 million Americans in 17 western states and provides 1 in 5 western farmers a source of irrigation for their crops. The world class trout fishing that exists on many of their 180 managed projects throughout the west is a byproduct of their original intended purpose, and falls a little farther down their list in the range of importance, and is treated as thus. To make things a little more fuzzy as far as our stretch of water goes, there's a plan called The San Juan River Basin And Recovery Implementation Program that is in execution here, that in a nutshell requires the BOR to maintain a target base flow of 500 to 1,000 cfs through the "critical endangered fish habitat area" from Farmington to Lake Powell for the recovery of the Colorado pike minnow and razorback suckers. Since this "critical" flow also relies upon water provided from the Animas River, when flows from the Animas (which is one of the few remaining free flowing rivers left in Colorado) drop, the difference must be compensated for by the only man-made regulated water source in the equation—the San Juan. Throw in the increased need for irrigation downriver, during hot summer months and there you have it—your 1,000 cfs San Juan flow. As for the "why now" part of it all, today's USGS Water Resources website shows flows on the Animas near Durango at 410 cfs and dropping—well below the 100 year average for this date of 2,520 cfs. So all in all, we can sleep a little easier tonight knowing that the pike minnows and suckers downstream are safe in the hands of the BOR, and that after a few days our fish will adjust once again and return to their normal eating habits before too long. Until then, you're going to have to burn a little wading boot leather and find the new spots they've moved to. Right now I'm seeing a lot of fish holding deep and they aren't moving around a lot, especially with a lot of food being carried right to them by the increased flows. I think your best bet to get their attention is going to be a recipe of more weight, an attractor like an egg pattern or San Juan worm, with a small dropper, especially of the red or cream larva, variety. The only real action I have seen for dry flies in recent days has been the bacchanalian type feast taking place during the last hour before dark on small midge patterns. If you can tough out the mosquitoes for the last hour, you can take a lot of fish on small adult midge patterns and end your day in grand style. I think we can forget about the caddis moving up or probably anywhere for a while. They like water in the high 40 to 50 degree range to really do their thing and this recent surge of cold water has probably put the kibosh on that. The fishing hasn't gone to hell in a hand basket by any stretch of the imagination, now that the flows have stabilized, the "catching" part should return in short order.

6/27/2011

I suppose most of us that fished the San Juan for the week following the high water, have been spoiled. The fishing was almost too easy and the fish were, just-well, acting stupid. They were rising to big crazy stuff--ants, hoppers, beetles, you name it. Well, it has become a little more difficult, lately; although there are still plenty of opportunities to catch fish, you just have to work at it a little harder. The water is gin clear right now and flowing at 470 cfs. The river bottom has been scoured of all the annoying didymo and you can see every rock in there, down to at least four feet. You would think that this would make for great fishing, and it did while the fish were on a heavy feed and spread out all over the river, after the high water. But most of these fish wised up real quick, and realized that they would quickly become a great target for ospreys, blue herons, and fly fishermen, if they continued to stay out in the shallow, clear water, where they were easy to spot. So the dynamic has changed a bit and a lot of the fish have moved to better cover in deeper runs, or in areas with darker moss colored backgrounds, where they are harder to spot. This is the type of water you should be targeting right now, if you are looking for numbers. With the bright sunshine and absence of any real hatches, you'll need to work the fishy-looking runs with the usual small midge patterns from size 24 down to size 28 with at least 6x tippet, fluorocarbon wouldn't hurt, either. Patterns like Krystal Flash, Scintilla Midge, Black Beauties, and Flouro Midges, are gonna work, you just have to find those runs that are holding fish and work them at the depths the fish are feeding, to be productive. Don't get me wrong; there are still some opportunities to take some nice fish on bigger dries, they're just not smacking them on every blind cast, like they were. I've had my best luck by finding those lone fish that are in a foot to three feet of water, holding higher in the water column and casting at least three feet in front of them--it helps if the water is moving at a moderate pace, I haven't been able to raise many fish in the faster water, like last week, and the slow stuff, just allows them to get too much time to inspect the fly, with the water being so clear. There has been some decent dry fly action on small midge patterns--Griffith Gnats, Fore and Afts, Black Adult Midges in the late afternoon, just after sunset and there has been some caddis activity in the p.m., from Crusher Hole, down. If you plan on staying late for this, I would highly recommend some bug spray right now, as the mosquitoes are beginning to get fired up. We're still waiting and keeping our fingers crossed for the emergence of the PMD's, hopefully we'll see those afternoon blanket hatches like we had last year, real soon. We'll keep you posted, if it happens; meanwhile, there's still some great fishing out there, while most of the other Western waters are still locked in runoff for several weeks, so it's a great time to visit the San Juan.

7/01/2012

It's so hot...... Well, you can fill in the blank. Hot and dry weather in the region mean that the San Juan continues to flow around 1,000 cfs and that translates to a change in the fishing dynamic, if you haven't fished here for a few weeks. The fish are still out there and they still have to eat, but the easy fishing days of fishing big dry foam patterns when the water level was 500 and 650 cfs are a thing of the past, for now. If you want catch these fish, you're going to have to work just a little harder at it and change your tactics a bit. For some fly fishermen, that is part of the enjoyment of the game. Being able to "read" the fish and the conditions and then finding that right combination to adapt, overcome, and fool those fish provides a certain feeling of accomplishment in knowing that you have used a bit of your experience and grey matter to unlock the mystery in the pursuit. I'll be the first to admit that I'm partial to catching my fish on dry flies, and especially on big terrestrial patterns that are easier to see, but you gotta play the hand you've been dealt sometimes, and as they say "When in Rome..." And sometimes in order to figure out what is going on, you need to figure out what is not. As for what is not, right now it's hatches (unless you count the last hour before dark, each day.) You're going to see a lot of fish "glued' to the bottom in deeper runs and they are not moving around a lot, for the main reason, that they don't have to. At 1,000 cfs they have a conveyer belt of food being delivered right to their doorstep. To get the interest of these fish you are going to have to get your offering right in front of their face and it's going to have to be something they are accustomed to eating. My recipe for unlocking the mystery was to think about what food sources go hand-in-hand with higher flows and I figured that small bits of moss (rich in bug life) and midge larva and pupa are generally being dislodged and more prevalent in the food chain than what we were seeing at 500 and 650 cfs. I was successful with rigging a small bead head olive woolly bugger and trailing it with a size 22 or 20 red larva, or cream UFO and dead drifting it under an indicator, adjusting my depth to keep it just off the bottom, to holding fish. Keep in mind that the further you move down the river, a greater prevalence of baetis nymphs exist, so you may want to exchange those midge patterns to ones that reflect what the fish are seeing and eating. The whole technique is kinda like watching sausage being made...the process isn't very pretty, but you can't argue with results. If you're fishing some of the shallower stuff, there have been good results, especially between 11:00 and 1:00 with small midge patterns like zebra midges and ju-ju's, but keep them small—like size 26 and 28—small. Just look at the size of the few midges are crawling on your waders during this time, and you'll see what I mean. We've received some reports that there are a lot of PMD nymphs present right now in the lower river, below the Quality Water Boundary and as of yesterday, there were some adults on the water. If you want to target these fish I can't think of a better pattern than a small Hare's Ear, fished under an indicator. Let's keep our fingers crossed that this hatch will migrate up river and we'll start seeing those epic PMD hatches we saw during 2:00 and 4:00 p.m. during the whole month of July, two years ago, and we can start throwing some PMD dries to these fish. For those dreamers out there, there's a 30% chance of thundershowers in the forecast for most days this week and if we get enough rain, we are ripe for a good ant fall. Until then, my motto is: You gotta do, what you gotta do, to catch fish—whatever works.

7/3/2011

Fishing on the San Juan right now, is not as easy as it can be at times. That said; it is also not what I would call, real tough. This river is; and probably will always be, a technical river. To me, that means that there times when you have to work a little to catch a satisfying number of fish, and I'm o.k. with that. Like they say, "If it were easy, everyone would be doing it." Since I fish this river a lot, I'm happy that I can go out some days and still be challenged on the water, figuring out the different flies and methods that work, is part of the allure of fly fishing. Sure, there are times when there are great hatches, or ant falls, when this river is easy, and anyone can catch a lot of fish with relative ease; but to me, that doesn't quite bring me the same satisfaction as having to use my grey matter a little to outsmart a creature with a brain the size of a pea. If I had a panacea for you right now that would unlock the secrets for the San Juan for this upcoming week; believe me, I would share it. I can; however, give you a few tips that will probably make your fishing here a little more productive. Here are the conditions we have seen for the past couple of weeks: bright clear skies with lots of warm New Mexico sunshine, no real hatches to speak of, gin clear water, and a clean, cobbled river bottom that makes fish a little harder to spot. Now, what to do about all that. Due to the nature of the bug life in this river, and the fact that the primary source of food for these fish consists mostly of small midges, they have to feed a lot to get the nutrition they need to survive; and that, my friends, is good news. Also, since the water is lower and clear, the fish are going to concentrate, where they can find two things, first food, then cover. So, armed with this information, the most productive spots to fish are going to be in the places where fish can hold and feed and not be spotted as easy prey for their natural predators. Look for fish in the deeper runs right now, especially in the seams of currents, where they have an abundance of food coming by and don't have to expend a lot of energy to get it, and where they feel safe, and can escape to deeper water, if they feel threatened. Also, fish the "thalwegs", of those runs. That's the scientific name for the main body of current that flows through the run, which in turn, carries the majority of food source to the fish. Be prepared to move a little. If you're continually fishing the same run, and using a lot of different offerings, and you feel pretty confident that your drifts are right, and you're still not hooking up, don't be afraid to try some new spots. Even the best fisherman, with the right flies, isn't going to catch fish, if there are no fish in the run. Concentrate on your drifts. When the fish get selective, you have to have your flies moving naturally at the proper speed, to get takes. Watch your indicator and notice if it is moving at the same speed as the bubbles or debris on the water, and if you can see the fish, watch them, as well. If you know that your flies are close to the fish and you see them make any sort of movement, set the hook, you'll be surprised at how many times, the fish actually had your fly and the indicator never moved, and you can always cast again, if it wasn't your fish. Adjust and adapt the location for your indicator and your weight. In order to catch these fish you need to get your flies in front of their face. This is going to require some experimentation on your part to get this dialed in and it's a lot easier if you can see where the fish are holding in the water column. Keep adjusting until you're confident you're getting it right. Use the flies that are known to be consistent producers, you know, the ones that always are a constant food source for these fish—small midge patterns, down to size 26 and even 28, and play around with the color offerings in black, grey and olive. Fish two different selections of flies. If one of these becomes the predominate producer, cut off the other, and fish two of the pattern that is working. Use 6x tippet, and 7x if you are fishing small dries. The water is very clear, and you need everything working to your advantage. Now, for the weather conditions for this upcoming week, it's going to be around 90 degrees every day, with a chance of thundershowers every day except Tuesday. If we get a significant rain, the conditions are great right now for an epic ant fall. If that happens, then you can forget everything I just told you, and go and get yourself some big foam ant patterns, and have some of the best and easiest dry fly fishing of your life. If not, then don't worry about the weather, and just get out there and enjoy yourself and catch, some of these beautiful San Juan fish. I think Anton Chekhov might have said this best—"People don't notice whether it's winter or summer, when they are happy."

7/8/2011

In my fishing report last week I suggested that if we saw a significant amount of rainfall during the week, we might possibly see the mythical "ant fall" that is so coveted by those that fish the San Juan. Well, Wednesday night we got the rain and on Thursday, the ants were out—not in prolific numbers; as in some years past, but in numbers enough to get the fish to feed pretty recklessly on big ant imitation patterns. While I'm sure I have a fair share of readers out there that view some of the advice and predictions of these reports with a certain degree of skepticism and incertitude, I would be remiss not to point out that "even a blind squirrel finds a nut sometimes." Skeptic or not, you would be hard pressed to argue that the event didn't produce some of the best dry-fly fishing so far this year. For me, fishing with big foam patterns to fish that have abandoned all their normal sensibilities is; no doubt, the pinnacle of the sport. I'm drawn to those visual images of a big trout drifting back and sizing up a dry fly and at that final moment of commitment when they slowly engulf it, when your mind and synapses must all come together in the precise moment of the lifting of the rod tip and your heart skips a beat, the whole world stops turning for just that moment, and you become tight to a fish. I'm drawn to it like a hillbilly to a banjo tune, there's just something about it that stirs the soul. I haven't lived in my native area of Appalachia for over 30 years and I've long since traded my overalls, straw-hat, and bare feet for waders, wading boots and ball cap, but I must confess that when I hear the intro of Foggy Mt. Breakdown, my feet involuntarily start tapping and I get a "hankering" for some of that old corn likker that the Artrip brothers used to run through the copper tubing up in the holler. Dry fly fishing this good is like that, it'll get in there and it's just gotta come out. This week, due to cooler, wet conditions, the BOR plans to scale back the releases here to 650 cfs on Monday at 9:00 a.m. I think we'll see more favorable conditions for fishing that in weeks past, when the water was around 1,000 cfs. If nothing else, you'll be able to sight fish a little easier and access more water, if you are wading. I would target the fish above Texas Hole, to Cable Hole, in the morning with small midge patterns like Ju-Ju's, Krystal Flash, and midge larva and pupae imitations—Fore and Afts, small Griffiths Gnats and even terrestrials if you see risers. Around 2:00 p.m. head down river where you're likely to see some Baetis activity, especially if we continue to have good cloud cover. There has been some PMD showing up in the lower river (they are big and easy to spot), but they haven't come off in significant enough numbers to get the fish very interested. They aren't as finicky to the weather conditions and I've seen some of the best hatches on bright, hot days, so keep a look out for a possible PMD hatch—it could still happen and when it does, the fishing is hard to beat.

7/10/2011

"Nobody goes there anymore, because it's too crowded."--Yogi Berra. Some folks that fished the San Juan back in the 80's and early 90's often refer to this quote as an explanation for why this river isn't nearly as crowded now, as it was back then. They claim that a big majority of people that used to travel here to fish now stay away due to the fact that they just grew tired of fighting the crowds, in what some referred to as "combat fishing". Others cite the nation's current economic conditions, and they reason that people now can no longer to afford the luxury of spending their hard earned discretionary income, on things such as fly fishing and the costs involved in traveling to distant locations to participate in the sport. Others espouse the theory, that once the luster of "The Movie", wore off, that the numbers of people involved in the sport, fell off and there just aren't as many people enamored by it anymore. I'm not really sure if it's any one of the above reasons, or a combination of them all, or none at all, but I am convinced that there are a lot less fishermen on this river than there were back then, and it's especially noticeable during the summer months, and it's definitely not because the quality or quantity of fish has diminished. Just his past week, I spent the major part of a week day in a spot on the river, where I fished dry flies to big fish and never saw another person, and the next afternoon, I fished a less secluded spot where the only other people I saw were in two boats that passed by 50 yards away. So, if you happen to be one of those folks that have never fished the San Juan, or you fished it in years past and now stay away because it's too crowded, you are missing out on the opportunity of enjoying one of the west's best trout fisheries. Of course the weekends are a bit busier than what you will find on, say a Monday or Tuesday, but even then I am able to find plenty of spots to fish, without standing shoulder to shoulder with a crowd. You'll never find the solitude here that you will experience on some back-country stream, but as on any tailwater worth its salt, that's never going to be possible.

Now; with all that said, here's what you can expect in the week to follow. The weather is going to be great, with temperatures in the high 80's and a chance of afternoon thundershowers, especially on Tuesday evening, which could bring on that epic ant fall that everyone keeps calling and asking about. I heard a few comments this past week that the fishing was "slow", but I was out on three separate occasions and caught plenty of fish and three of them were probably my best fish this year. Yes the water is clear, and the flow is around 500 cfs, and the fish aren't holding in most of those super easy spots where you can catch them with little effort, but they are still out there, and they still need to eat. There aren't any prolific hatches going on right now, but the small midge patterns such as Krystal Flash in size 26 and 28 are still bringing plenty of fish to the net. Other patterns such as the Mono Midge, Scintilla Midge, Abe's Silk Midge, Cream UFOs, and Red Naked Ladies are working, as well. Grey, seems to be the predominate color, but I'm hearing it helps to be flexible and change flies as you move to new spots and during different times of the day, to consistently catch fish. Ants, beetles, and hoppers are also working well right now and fishing a sunken Black Epoxy Ant, below a hopper pattern has been especially effective. The terrestrial patterns seem to be working well along the banks and shallower riffles, since fish in the deeper runs are holding further down in the water column. I think the key to success with terrestrials right now, is to keep moving and put them in front of as many fish as you can. It's not like standing in one spot and continuously nymphing a run. Find some fish and work them, if you get snubbed, move on to new fish, you won't be able to force feed them. Most of my experience has shown that they are usually gonna take it on the first of second pass, or they (ant). We're still looking for the PMDs to start any day, and once that happens, we're talking about dry fly fishing on a whole different level. Also; as mentioned above, we have a pretty decent shot at an ant fall, if those afternoon showers bring some significant rain. Great weather, great fishing, no big crowds--if that sounds like your idea of fun, then it's time for a trip to the San Juan.

7/17/2011

"So easy, a caveman could do it." That's how I would describe the fishing from this past Wednesday. We had a heavy rain shower on Tuesday evening on the upper river and although it didn't last very long it was enough to produce a pretty decent ant fall. By 9 a.m. the fish had begun to key in on the big protein offerings; that didn't quite carpet the river, but were numerous enough to get most of the fish looking up. As I walked down the river from Texas Hole, I saw nearly every boat in the area hooked up with a fish, on an ant pattern and proceeded to do so myself to virtually every fish I saw that was holding higher in the water column or in the shallows. Even later in the day, when the ants became more scarce, I found lots of fish still willing to rise to big foam ant patterns, and this continued on into Thursday, as well. While I will be the first to say that sort of dry fly fishing is somewhat of an anomaly, it sure is a lot of fun when it does happen. Now, for this upcoming week you can expect some hot weather reaching the mid 90's, with a slight chance of thundershowers each day as the clouds begin to build in the evening. A decent shower would cause a repeat of last week's ant fall, but most of the weather we have been seeing recently has only produced a lot of clouds in the afternoon and very little precipitation. So, the conditions you are most likely to find will be lots of bright sunshine, gin clear water around 500 cfs, with some very sparse midge hatches that occasionally occur around 11:00 to 1:00 p.m. If this sounds like a repeat of what you have been hearing about the fishing conditions here for the last few weeks, it's because--well, it is. So the methods for taking fish right now are going to pretty much stay the same. A lot of areas on the river are fishing like a big spring creek and the clarity and speed of the water are going to require that you are on top of your game to catch the number of fish you normally expect from the San Juan. I'm not saying that the fishing is slow right now; just that it's not the "no-brainer" fishing it can sometimes be. So, you're gonna have to work at it a little and use 6x tippet, very light weight, and very small midge patterns when you nymph. Stick to the "fishy" looking runs of slightly deeper water, and be prepared to move a little more to find fish. As far as patterns, I think some of the best picks right now are small Scintillas in black, Krystal Flashes in size 26 and 28's, and Mono Midges, in that order. If you do find some rising fish, it's more than likely going to be to tiny midges and the best pattern for this is the Fore And Aft in size 24, fished on a long leader tapered down to 7x fluorocarbon. Hoppers, ants, and beetles are still producing some fish, but the key to this is finding the right fish, so you will need to show these flies to as many different fish as you can to produce numbers. There has been some PMD activity in the lower river, below Crusher Hole, although the hatches are still very light right now. PMD nymphs are taking some fish in this area, but I haven't heard of any great action on dries yet. I have been seeing a few of the adults below Texas Hole this past week, but not enough to get the fish interested, so far. This however, could be the week that we could start seeing them come off in numbers that they will start to become a target for the fish. I think it's time to start watching the Simon Canyon/Durangler's Corner area during the afternoon, for further developments on this. All in all, there's still plenty of good fishing out there, with a decent chance of it becoming epic, at any moment, depending on the weather.

7/22/2012

Hey Bureau Of Reclamation, you're making me look bad here. I caught some flack in the shop this past week for reporting from a BOR e-mail I had received that Friday, that they intended to take the San Juan flow down to 650 cfs, on Monday, and it actually ended up closer to 800 cfs. In their defense, I will note the caveat that they did include was: that this was a projected flow and was predicated on their forecast for an increase in the Animas River due to expected rainfall. Sometime between Friday and Monday, someone made an executive decision and 13 minutes before the 9:00 a.m. release change on Monday, they sent out another e-mail, announcing that the flow would actually be closer to 800 cfs. Don't shoot me; I'm just the piano player. The USGS page for the Animas flow in Durango, shows the river at 286 cfs this morning and dropping, so I wouldn't look for any changes in the San Juan releases in the downward range, for a while. There's the chance for an increase here to 1,000 cfs if the Animas continues to drop, but hey, I'm not even gonna touch that one. It would be easier to pass myself off as a financial analyst and tell you what the stock market is going to do for the next 6 months, than to play water-prognosticator and make predictions on what actions the BOR is going take for the rest of the summer. I can; however, report that after the dust settled on Monday, the fishing picked up for the week and we began to see some better hatches and more active feeding from the fish. Was it due to the drop in the water? My limited knowledge of entomology doesn't qualify me here for a treatise on that, so I'll just quote the father character in the movie "Joe Dirt" and say, "Hey! How exactly is a rainbow made? How exactly does the sun set? How exactly does a posi-trac rear end on a Plymouth work? It just does." So, I'll take it—better hatches, better fishing, all fine by me. The midges we are seeing are still small, but the good news is that we're seeing more of them and the hatches are lasting longer. I've been noticing a lot of fish are on to the emergers, with dorsal and caudal fins on the surface for hours at a time and there have been good reports on effective fishing, targeting them with black Krystal Flash patterns, Ju-Jus, and Scintillas, in sizes 26 and smaller, fished shallow in the surface film. Once the adults appear in numbers you can start targeting them with Fore and Afts, single Adult Midge patterns, and small Griffith's Gnats. The water is super clear right now, so I'll suggest that you go down to a 7x tippet, for those small dries. Further down the river, we are seeing good afternoon hatches of PMDs with a mix of Baetis and the dry fly fishing there has really picked up, especially on Comparadun imitations of either species. Nymphing with Hare's Ears and small Baetis nymphs has been effective in the hours before the hatch kicks off. We've been having our fair share of afternoon thundershowers and the wash at Simon Canyon has been a spoiler for some of this downstream fishing, and on some afternoons; if the rain is heavy, the wash blows out and the lower river turns to chocolate milk. The storms have been short in duration; for the most part, and if you can stick them out, there has been some fantastic fishing in the evenings after the wind and rain dies down. Just as a tube top is considered "haute couture" at a redneck wedding; if you're headed here this week, a rain jacket would be a nice addition to your wardrobe.

1/24/2011

A gentleman named Lee Wulff; that was no doubt a much better fisherman than myself, once said, "The last thing to change is the fly." I think there is a lot of truth to that statement, and it especially applies to the San Juan, right now. During the course of the week, I fish this river a little, and I have a lot of conversations with guides, and fishermen of all skill levels, that visit the shop. It seems that most have varying opinions on which flies are most effective, but most are steadfast in their convictions that they have unlocked the mystery of the secret fly for our present fishing conditions, and they run the gamut from streamers, to tiny midge patterns, cartoon hoppers, chamois leeches, and even San Juan worms. So who's right? Well, in a way--they all are. I think that while matching the hatch is important, that a mediocre fly choice; fished properly, will trump the right bug, most of the time, as long as it's not too ridiculous. In my own experience, confidence in your fly choice counts for a lot, and if you can find the spots where the fish are and get the depth and the delivery speed right, you will have most of the problem licked. However, with the conditions of clear water, and lower flows; that exist right now, it helps to have some information at your disposal to increase your chances at catching fish, which is why people read columns like this. So, what can I tell you here that would help? My advice would be the following: stick with small midge larva/pupa patterns in sizes 26 and 28, especially in olive and brown (it's the primary food source from the Texas Hole on up). Use 6x fluorocarbon tippet and small weight from size 8 even down to 9. Pay close attention to where the fish are feeding in the water column, and adjust your indicator accordingly--don't be afraid to move that thing up to a foot or two from your top fly, if the conditions dictate it. Use smaller, less obtrusive indicators--you don't need a beach ball to float a couple of size 28's and a #9 split shot, and these fish are becoming a little wary right now. Walk around a little, take your time, and find the fish. Now is the time to use those expensive polarized glasses you bought online last winter, when you were bored and couldn't fish, but couldn't stop thinking about it either. The water is so clear right now, that you can see most of the holding fish anywhere in the river, if you take a few moments and really concentrate on movement and shapes that represent fish. Sure, some people just walk out to "fishy looking" spots and cast before studying the water, and sometimes they hook up, but as they say, "even a blind squirrel finds a nut sometimes." Use the clear water to your advantage and pick out an individual fish and work him, watch for those subtle movements that represent a take and be ready to set the hook, if you misread him, you can always re-cast. There have been some decent midge hatches taking place the past couple of weeks, but they seem sporadic and you can't really set your watch by them, they seem to start and stop all throughout the day, but they are pretty unmistakable once they get going and the fish start to notice. I have picked up several fish by switching it up to a Fore And Aft size 24; while this is going on, and it seems to help a lot if if I go down to a 7x tippet on these small flies. As far as the lower river goes, there has been some decent fishing during mid-day on Baetis and PMD nymphs, although there hasn't been much in the way of hatches for either, lately. Rs2's, small Flashback Pheasant Tails, Chocolate and Grey Foamwings, and even little Hare's Ears are taking fish from the lower flats down past Durangler's Corner. There was a recent stocking down in this area, so if you're looking more for action than size, that might be a good place to concentrate your efforts for something a little different. I haven't given up hope for a good PMD hatch in the lower river just yet, but I beginning to have my doubts if it's going to really happen this year with the intensity it did last year. We'll keep our eyes out for this to happen, but I'm concerned that we may be running out of time for it to really get going. Overall, the entire river is still fishing surprisingly well, and although it been really hot and the mosquitoes are kinda bad, it's still really tough to beat this river right now for numbers and size of fish, if you put a little effort into it.

7/29/2012

A fly-fishing writer much more eloquent than I, is credited with the quote that "a river never sleeps." Roderick Haig-Brown made that statement many years ago and never were more true words spoken or more fitting in describing what happens on the San Juan during the summer months. There are differing schools of thought that emerge when considering this truism, and they range from seeing it as either a blessing, or a curse, depending on the fisherman. For those attempting to "match the hatch" at any particular time, at any particular area, under any particular set of weather conditions, this can be seen as a source of much frustration, while those that prefer to fish the garden variety of tried and true patterns; regardless of what's going on, can often be the beneficiary of 'hitting it just right" on some occasions, just through sheer perseverance. Even a broken clock is right two times a day. A fishing report that tells you what to fish, and where, and when; on a river with biomass as diverse as the San Juan, can at its best, serve as a generic guide. There's just a lot more going on out there that most of us will ever admit to knowing or seeing, to be entirely specific and right 100% of the time. Hell, I've seen it pour rain on one section of this river, while another remained as dry as powder. You can't tell me the same set of circumstances applies to both of those conditions. So with all that in mind, I'm going to share some of my "generic" observations from my recent fishing experiences, and those garnered from friends and acquaintances, whose opinions I trust. The way I see it now, is to focus on the midge activity in the morning, beginning with small (size 26 to 28) pupa and larva patterns in grey, olive, black and red, until you start to see some emerger activity, in the form of proposing rises, when you'll have to switch to emerger patterns like Krystal Flash, Ju-Jus, and Scintillas, to mimic that specific part of the hatch. Later; usually around 11:00, you can change over to midge dry patterns, once you start seeing the adults in significant enough numbers to get the fish focusing on them. This hatch isn't sparse, but it is short in duration, so you'll have about 45 minutes to an hour to experience some good dry fly fishing. My favorite pattern for this is the Fore and Aft, or a single adult midge pattern, in black, in sizes 24 and 26; respectively, both fished on 7x fluorocarbon tippet. During the mid-day hours, you'll start see a lot of fish gather in the main current, holding at depths of 2 to 4 feet and that's the time to go back to those pupa patterns in grey and black. You'll be able to see their feeding activity, telegraphed by their up and down and side to side motion, and getting your depth right with a good presentation is going to be the difference between hooking up, or not hooking up. This generic advice will cover you on a large portion of the river, from Texas Hole up to Cable Hole. Below that, you'll have to figure in the existence of Baetis and PMD nymphs into your equation and include some Fluff Baetis, Pheasant Tails, Grey Foam Wings, and Hare's ears into your arsenal, with a big focus on the Grey Foam Wings. "Getting it right", is going to depend on your ability to read what is happening with the fish and their reaction to the changes in the stages of emergence of either of these particular insects. The "no brainer hatch" of PMDs from Simon Point to the bait water section, looks like it is pretty much on its way out. I arrived down there last Monday; just as the clock struck 2:00, with full anticipation of fishing some of those big Emphemerella dun imitations to rising fish, only to find just a few bugs on the water for the next few hours and fewer fish rising for them. I later commented to a guide friend of mine that it looked to me that this hatch was over for the season and he told me that he heard from a reliable source that it was still going strong, but occurring later in the afternoon, than in weeks past. I'm not one for basing my fishing on third hand "intel", so I guess I'll have to go down there in the evenings and see for myself. If it is over, it sure was fun while it lasted. Around 4:00 or so, the midges usually get going again and you will start to see lots of takes in the surface film. With the afternoon cloud cover we've been seeing on most days, this can last right up until it gets too dark to see a fly, or an indicator. Most of these fish seem to be focusing on the emerging insects, rather than the adults; which is usually the case during any hatch, since they present an easier target for a trout as they struggle from their nymphal shucks and pose little danger of flying away. You can fool a few fish during this time with a dry fly, but you'll see better success if you focus your attention on emerger patterns and "stuck in the shuck" patterns, such as Buzzers, fished in the top 12 inches of water, or so. You can also, still prowl the back channel shallows, banks, and slack water and pick up some fish on ant patterns, but most of those fish in the main channels of water aren't having any part of that game right now.

8/5/2012

Being the eternal pessimist that I am, it's always my nature to see the glass as half empty. It's a trait that often robs me of ability to fully enjoy the true blessings that I do have, and allow myself to just live in the moment and appreciate things for what they are; rather than dwell on the dread I create, thinking about how I'm going to really miss it when it's gone. Despite the fact that we are still in our summer season here, I can't resist noticing those little signs like a few yellowing leaves on the willows along the river, or the fact that darkness is coming on a little earlier each day, and those back to school ads, that stir in me the thoughts of demise for my favorite time of year. Already, I find myself out on the water with my mind wandering towards thoughts of bugling elk, cool, crisp mountain mornings, and golden aspen leaves, when I should be focusing on the fishing that is before me. And, as if that isn't enough, I allow my cynical feelings and morose reflections of the season that follows, to creep in, with thoughts of snow, cold, and fewer hours to do the thing I love most. I'm probably the only guy on the river right now that can stand out there in the ninety degree heat and ruminate on how much I am going to hate doing this, wearing gloves and three layers of fleece. If anything positive can come from it at all, perhaps I will garner a greater regard for the pleasure of fishing the San Juan during summer and try to extract every last ounce of gratification possible from the remaining days of the season. And there are plenty of those opportunities out there now, for the taking. With flows near 800 cfs and crystal clear water conditions there is still plenty of time to get in some great sight fishing with midge pupae and larva in the mornings. As the day progresses, you'll start to see the fish move up in the water column for emerging midges around 10:30 to 11:00 a.m., and I've been doing well with ermerger imitations such as, Krystal Flash and Ju-Jus in grey and black in sizes 26 and 28. Immediately following this, there is a short window of opportunity for some dry fly action on small adult midge patterns, my favorite being the Fore and Aft in size 24. This hatch doesn't last very long, but if you are a dry fly fisherman, it's an opportunity you don't want to miss. On most days you'll have a chance to see it again in the upper river around 4:00 or 5:00 p.m. and it intensifies as the evening comes on. There are still fish rising to PMDs in the lower river and if you want to experience this, you need to be in place by around 1:30, when it starts to kick off and really gets going from around 2:00 till 4:00. By San Juan standards, these Emphemerella duns are big bugs and what I refer to as the Dolly Partons of our dry flies, because they ride big and high on the water. A size 16 PMD comparadun is a good imitation, but lately I found that I'm having better results fishing cripples, like Quigley's Cripple and Film Critics, especially to fish that have been pressured pretty heavily for the past few weeks. Trout also target these emerging insects with a little more conviction, since a struggling insect that can't yet fly and escape, presents itself as a better target than one that could possibly leave the surface at any moment. Lately my usual routine is to focus on the upper river and the midges until around 1:00 or 1:30, then hightail it downriver, switch flies, and wait for Dolly Parton. Once this hatch is finished out, I head back upriver and fish midge dries until I can't see my fly anymore, then head home. Whatever your routine is, the fact remains that we still have a good deal of great weather and fishing ahead, despite the fact that fall, and then winter, will be here before I am ready to accept either of them.

8/7/2011

"When the sun is bright and the moon is right, the fish will bite. Maybe"- Izaak Walton. That little tidbit was written back in the 1600's and there's still a lot of truth in that today. I'm not so sure about the moon this next week, but I do know that the sun will most likely be bright. It looks like we will have nothing but sunshine for the better part of the week, with the highs in the 90's, and maybe a chance of afternoon thundershowers on Saturday and Sunday. As far as fishing goes on the San Juan right now, it's about as technical as it gets. Bright sunshine, crystal clear water, and big smart fish that have seen about every fly pattern, known to mankind. As we head into the dog-days of summer, when a lot of people say these fish get lockjaw, you are going to have to step up your game a bit to keep your catch rate up, but it can be done and regardless of what some may think, these fish still have to feed often, due to the fact that the majority of their diet consists of small midges right now. What you are probably not going to see this week are any prolific Baetis, or PMD hatches, or Ant falls, that can make fishing conditions on this river, easy. However, there have been some midge hatches; especially in the Cable Hole and Upper flats area, around 11:00 am that really get the fish going for a while and you can pick off a good number of fish on size 24 Fore and Afts and size 26 Black Adult Midge patterns, but you need to go down to 7x tippet and present the best drift you've got in your repertoire. Just remember that by this time of the year, these fish have seen a lot of offerings from a lot of other fishermen and don't suffer bad casts, or poor presentations, very well. There have also been some good hatches in the afternoons around 4:00 and 5:00; depending on the nature of the fish gods, and these have been more pronounced when they happen, producing some larger midge clusters, and also lasting a little longer in their duration. As the hatch winds down, I have been pretty successful in seeking out those lone fish that; like me, just can't leave enough of a good thing alone, and continue to rise to the few midges left on the water. These "extra" fish can sometimes turn an ok day into a great one, if you don't mind moving around a little and actively seeking them out, and I sometimes find them easier to catch than those rising during heavy hatch conditions. One thing to note here, is that it's important to approach all these rising fish right now from above their holding positions and keep your leader and tippet out in front of them at an angle, they don't tolerate a fly line or leader going over their heads, with the water this low and clear. When you can't find any noticeable heads above the water, the smaller midge patters in grey and olive like size 26 Crystal Flash, Mono Midges, and UFO's are working well. There have also been good reports on small red Midge Larva, taking a good number of fish, too. Keep the tippets small, 6x is good, 7x is better, but it does make the landing part just a little harder. So, if you can get out here this week--do it! I already saw ads for back-to-school sales, and the smell of roasted chilies will soon fill the air, signaling the beginning of the end to what always seems to me, a too short summer season. As Sparse Grey Hackle once said- "Trout do not rise in the cemetery, so you better do your fishing while you are still able."

8/12/2012

Occasionally; my wild streak still comes out and I'll get an idea in my head and act on it, before the sensible side of my brain can act and spoil all the fun associated with those types of questionable decisions, with likewise questionable outcomes. So, the other night I threw a bunch of camping and fishing equipment into the back of the 4-Runner, loaded up the dog and a big thermos of coffee, and headed out during the wee morning hours, for a river past our state's northern border that is known for its very large, but difficult, and picky fish. After negotiating a few mountain passes and dodging various forms of wildlife associated with such regions, the coffee wore off a bit, and I found myself wondering if perhaps the night had written a check that the daylight wouldn't be able to cash. But after a glimpse or two of some crystal clear flowing water and the sound of the rushing stream from my open window, my sense of adventure was renewed by visions of those big trout in the bottom of my landing net. Overall, it did me a world of good to see that I hadn't lost my appetite for spontaneity and exploit, when it comes to fishing. After about an hour into the nuts and bolts of the actual fishing part, my indicator disappeared into the abyss of a deep run and when I lifted my rod tip, a brown trout the size of a large log drifted to the surface and gave me the evil eye. Fighting back initial panic, a surprisingly short fight ensued and before you know it I had wrangled the biggest trout I have ever hooked, to within ten feet below me into the shallows. With the line tight and the fish seemingly under my control, I reached for my net and the size 24 hook came unbuttoned, and I watched my fish of a lifetime give me a tail wag and an adios as he disappeared back into deeper water. Something inside me came unglued during that moment, and although I caught some other "decent" fish that day and the next, I just couldn't get my heart into the whole enterprise, the way I had before that incident occurred. The boss offered to cover for me for an extra day and although I knew the right thing to do would be to climb back on the bucking horse that threw me, I felt that what I really needed to do was tuck my tail between my legs and head back to my home waters on the San Juan, lick my wounds, and get some "piscatorial healing." Now I don't know if your reasons for coming here right now will reach as deep into your psyche as mine, but I can tell you that you can expect to have ample opportunities for some healing of your own. The flows have recently increased to around 922 cfs, and after a day or so of turbidity, the water has cleared considerably and sight fishing conditions have returned. Small gray midge patterns and gray foam wings seem to be the most consistent producers, if nymphing is your game and you can still find fish rising to midge adults during the midmorning hatch around 10:30 or 11:00, but most of these fish seem to be hugging the sides, out of the faster current. The BWO's aren't around in any numbers right now, and I wouldn't expect to see any of that activity, until this hot weather breaks and we see cooler fall conditions. Surprisingly enough; though, the PMDs on the lower river are hanging in there and you can still see some hatches in that area between 2:00 and 4:00 p.m. Late afternoon until dark you can expect to see another resurgence of midges and this time offers some good emerger and dry fly opportunities, to finish out your day. If you are looking for action on terrestrial patterns, I would stick to the back channels or tight to the banks on the main river, for those foam ants, beetles, and hoppers. All in all, the San Juan's a good place to be and a good place to relax and vanquish those old ghosts that you know are probably gonna haunt you for a while.

8/14/2011

Boy, we've got it good out here. Crystal clear water, lots of big fish, beautiful scenery, and great weather, I could go on and on. I had to travel north this past week to take care of some business just across the state line and decided to make a short visit to the freestone up there, because it was convenient and it had been a while since I had fished different water. While this is a beautiful river in its own right and I caught fish, they just weren't as large or numerous as what I have grown accustomed to on the San Juan. Now don't get me wrong, there's nothing wrong with fishing places other than your home waters, it helps keep your skills sharp, and I think life is all about adventure, anyway. But when I got back in the car and headed back home to the Juan, I kinda felt like I had just cheated on my girlfriend; that is, if I really had one right now. Hey, it's hard to cultivate and maintain any type of long- term relationship, when you spend all your spare time out in the middle of a river. Anyway; although I must admit that I am a little spoiled and biased, I just think that for great overall fly-fishing destinations it's hard to beat the San Juan, especially in the summer. So, what's going on out here right now? Well, the flow here was bumped up earlier in the week from 500 cfs to around 800 cfs, to compensate for the decreased water levels in the Animas, and provide for more irrigation water headed downstream. More than likely these levels will stay the same until we see the first frost in the area, signaling the end of the need for irrigation water, or if the Animas watershed starts getting a lot of rain and raises water levels there. For the first day or so of the 800 cfs flow, there was a slight increase in the amount of moss and debris in the main channel of the river, and the fish were moving around a little to adjust to the change of currents that pushed the food source to different areas that existed at 500 cfs, but they found their new lies pretty quick and the water cleared up and things were back to normal, in short order. One noticeable change, was that the side channels seemed to hold a lot more fish than what I had been seeing during the lower flows. As far as fly patterns go, there really hasn't been much of a change in that department: midge patterns in olive and grey and small midge dry patterns, when you see the risers. I did hear several good reports of larger midge patterns like Tav's Big Mac in brown, taking several good fish this week, so that is worth a look. The afternoon hatches around 4:00

and 5:00 have been the heaviest of the day and have produced some good midge clusters that have offered some nice opportunities to fish larger midge dry patterns, even in the Dead Chicken variety. I'm still catching fish on foam ant patterns in size 14 and 12 and it has been my experience that this will continue to work until the leaves start to fall, if you stick to those fish that are holding in the shallow riffles, or tight against the banks. The weather for the upcoming week looks to be warm, with quite a few chances for afternoon thundershowers and some cloud cover, and there could be a chance for some baetis to appear, although I wouldn't hold my breath on that one. The prolific PMD hatch that we saw last summer that lasted for over a month, just doesn't look like it will repeat itself this year and I'm just not enough of an entomologist to figure out why, although I am a little heartbroken that I won't have the opportunities to fish big dry PMD patterns to fish that feed with reckless abandon. I guess it just goes to show you that this river is just like any other beautiful woman, there are times when she can bring you sheer bliss, but other moments when she can just break your heart.

8/19/2012

Goose poop and mosquitoes. I still stay in limited contact with a few friends of mine from those days of working in the big cities up and down the east coast of the U.S. and from time to time they comment on their envy of my trout-bum, seemingly carefree lifestyle. I never really bother to point it out to them, but what they don't see is the less glamorous side of my way of life and all those vicissitudes I must daily endure in the pursuit, thereof. It's easy to say you would gladly give up being stuck in bumper to bumper traffic for the opportunity to be standing knee deep in the crystal clear rushing waters of a world-class trout stream, under a big bluebird western sky, tossing dry flies to big rising fish. But would you really trade in your chilled- gazpacho- and —rare —ahi- steak- with- garlic- aioli- and- Pellegrino- water- lunch in a comfortable, air conditioned downtown restaurant, for my cold- ham —and- cheese- sandwich- and- lukewarm- water- from the tap at Abe's, if you had to hurry and wolf it down on a little goose poop covered island while swatting mosquitoes in 100 degree heat, because the fish are rising to PMDs out there and you can't waste time on something as trivial as food right now? Would you be willing to give up that double-pump-mocha-latte at Starbucks and swap it for the last remaining dregs of yesterday's coffee from a 20 year old stainless steel thermos, because you drove all night over one of the most treacherous highways in the lower 48 and the nearest form of a coffee shop is at least an hour away, just to fish? Be careful what you wish for my friends—"Uneasy lies the head that wears a crown." Despite having to endure such tribulations to do so, I managed to make it out on the water here for a few days this past week and receive my just rewards. Depending on who you're talking to, the fishing is good right now. After a somewhat sluggish morning on Monday, I had a great day on size 16 ant patterns, in the back channels. So great; that I never made it out to the main river as I had intended, because it just didn't make sense to go looking for fish when they were cooperating right in front of me. On Tuesday, I found fish rising in the morning and managed to take them on a size 24 Fore and Aft pattern and when that cooled off, I went headhunting for big fish in the shallows and those holding high in the water column with a parachute hopper pattern. Somewhere around 4 p.m. the hopper bite really turned on and the fishing was hotter than a $2 pistol for an hour and a half to 2 hours. And it wasn't any of that casual, midge sipping, type of dry fly fishing—no sir, this was one of those deals when the fish took the fly with more conviction than a Baptist preacher at an old time tent revival. The kind of take that looks and sounds more like a toilet bowl flushing, than the rise of a trout. Twice, I caught fish while my hopper was underwater downstream, with my rod between my knees, fumbling in my waist pack for something or other. Now I can't say if this week will be a repeat of that performance, but I can guarantee you I'm going to try. As for advice on everything else, if you like the nymphing game there's been some pretty good fishing in the earlier morning hours when the midges are more active, on gray and chocolate foam wings from Texas hole and below. Up higher it's gray and black Crystal Flash, Ju-Ju's and Scintillas until mid-day and the fish start hugging the bottom, then the strategy will have to change with more weight and depth with pupa and larva patterns. I'll be the first to admit that the hopper thing is something of an anomaly on this river and it sort of comes and goes in short windows of opportunity without any precursors. My only advice on that type of fishing is that you have to just give it a go and see if it works, if you hit it right, your fishing is gonna be memorable. The flows are still around 920 cfs and most of the fish I am seeing are on the sides and in slower shallower runs out of the current, if that helps a bit. The river's not crowded, especially during the week days, and the weather is great, although the mosquitoes; as well as the goose poop, are still around.

8/21/2011

Rocky Ford melons, Hatch green chilies, Olathe corn, and Palisade peaches--harvest time in the Rockies is one of those palate pleasing times that I truly love, but also brings me mixed feelings of sadness, because it is a harbinger of the end of another summer season and the long days in the pursuit of my piscatorial pleasures. Yeah, I know fall is a beautiful season for fishing out here; but in my opinion, it's way too short and I seem to enjoy it less as I grow a little older, because all I can focus on is what is to come and it brings forth thoughts of the long cold days of winter, when I spend time knocking the ice out of the guides of my fly rod. I guess I'm one of those hopeless pessimists that always see the glass half full, no matter what. But, we've still got several warm summer days left to enjoy on the river out here, so in the words of Janis Joplin, my attitude is-- "You better get it while you can." This coming week is going to be one of those weeks, weather-wise. We can expect highs in the lower 90's with a slight chance of isolated thundershowers in the afternoons, typical everyday stuff for northern New Mexico in late August and early September. As far as water conditions go, we had a bump this past week in the flow levels to around 900 cfs to compensate for the decreased flow in the Animas and provide needed water downstream for the endangered Razorback Sucker and Squawfish or Pike Minnow. Lots of people that fish here, just love these levels, but I'm not one of them. I tend to fish a lot of dries and find that this level reduces the number of places I prefer to sight fish for big trout, holding in shallow water, sipping small midges. However; the fishing is still very good, I'm just a creature of habit and like to fish all my favorite spots, rather than spend the time to find where they have moved to, when the water changes. We all have our own personal preferences. I guess that any effort to preserve a fish species should be applauded these days, but I once saw a Razorback Sucker and a Pike Minnow in the Denver Aquarium; I wasn't that impressed, and any fish's diminished propensity to take a fly, moves it a little down the chain of importance in the ecosystem for me. Besides, I don't think I'd be particularly interested in catching any fish that has the words, sucker or minnow, in its name. So, now I'll get off my soap box and tell you what's going on, here on the Juan. Surprise!, it's still small midges. Patterns of grey Crystal Flash midges, olive Monomidges, cream and red Larva in sizes 24 to 28's are still working well, and Fore and Afts, black Adult Midges, and Griffith's Gnats in sizes 24 and smaller, when you see the risers. There hasn't been a real predictable pattern to the midge hatches, but for the most part they have been occurring between 11:30 and 1:00 and then again around 4:30 or 5:00 in the afternoon, however; the opportunity to fish the later hatches with dries has been negated on most days by the wind, which seems to be the only thing we are getting from the storms that build up later in the day. Ant patterns are still working on enough fish to keep me interested in throwing them, but I'm having better luck with that on the solitary fish in shallow water, or the one's holding tight against the banks. There was a day this past week when we had a nice Baetis hatch that lasted several hours and the fish were on the feed, with a lot of heads coming up, but it seemed to be somewhat of an anomaly, and I couldn't begin to tell you what triggered it. Anyway, I wouldn't want to be unprepared out there if it happens again this week, so I would have some Comparaduns and Sparkle Duns in size 22 in my box, just in case. There's no bigger disappointment than when it's raining soup and you're the only one standing there holding a fork. My advice is to get out here and enjoy the great summer weather and fishing that we still have left for this season and on your trip out you might want to stop at one of those roadside fruit and vegetable stands and pick up some of the delicious bounty this part of the country offers around this time each year.

8/26/2012

Go early and stay late. That pretty much sums up my advice for fishing the San Juan right now. Having this river a stone's throw from my front door has, no doubt, made me a little complacent and lazy in my approach to fishing it lately. When you know that you can go out at pretty much anytime of the day and still get into some quality fish, you sometimes lose your edge and don't approach it with the zeal you once had when the opportunity was a little harder to come by. It's a little easier to have that extra cup of coffee and stay a little longer at the shop, BSiing with everyone, when you really should be on the water, making the most of every day. I'm spoiled and I know it. I came to this realization the other day after I spent the morning lollygagging around and finally managed to get on the water at the early crack of 9:30, to find fish rising everywhere to a morning midge hatch. I wasted no time fishing tiny midge patterns to rising fish for the next 45 minutes or so, but I couldn't help wondering how long this had been going on before I got there and how much of it I had missed. That's what happens when you think you know too much. This week I think I'll put a little more hustle into my routine and show a little more respect for the blessing of having this gem of a river at my doorstep. Now I don't mean--break of day early--but, no more 9:30 stuff, until it starts to get a lot colder in the mornings. The staying late thing, I have never had a problem with. As a matter of fact, I caught some of my best fish this past week when I stayed, what some would consider too late, twitching a hopper pattern to rising fish that gave me some explosive takes, well past what a sane person would consider dark. So I paid for it with having to make three attempts to cross the channel I was on and I floundered around a little in the bushes on my way out with the mosquitoes--it was worth it. I like that time out there, alone as you could ever feel, just you and these fish, the lonesome hum of tires from the oilfield trucks on their way home, blocked out by your concentration on that last rising fish and the familiar buzz of a mosquito that, like you, refuses to quit. If you come out this week, expect to find the flows around 1,000 cfs. and clear water conditions. My guess is that the flows are going to stay around 1,000 cfs to 900 cfs until later in October, when the need for irrigation water diminishes. If you want to know what's going on with San Juan flows, just look at the USGS site for the flows of the Animas river in Colorado. Today at the Durango gauging station it's flowing at 230 cfs--well off it mean value of 430 for this time of year. As I mentioned earlier, there's some good midge activity earlier in the mornings--unfortunately I can't tell you until next week how early it starts, but I do know it's going on before 9:30 and it appears to taper off by 11:00. Small midge dries on 7x tippet and midge emerger patterns, especially in gray and black, like Krystal Flash, Ju-Jus, and Scintillas, under an indicator with 6x, should get you into fish, during this time. Later on, midge larva and pupa patterns, fished a little deeper are the ticket when the fish drop back down in the water column. I have been filling in what a lot of people refer to as "the down time" of the day with some good terrestrial fishing, especially with hoppers and ant patterns. I am really partial to the Schroeder's Parachute Hopper pattern with a tan body, especially when fished in transitional water, the so called "seams" between fast and slower moving currents. You can also pick up some nice fish by tossing some ants and hoppers near the banks, which is a good thing right now with these flows, because I'm seeing a lot of fish holding there, out of the current. There are a few baetis out there right now in the morning, but not really enough to get the fish looking up for them. The nymphs; however, are present and gray foam wings and olive CDC RS2's are a must have, if you're fishing below Texas Hole. The PMDs are really a thing of the past, with a few showing up here and there, but not in any numbers to get the fish excited about them. After the sun drops behind the hills, you can target those fish in the slower moving water, with some hopper patterns, as they begin to rise to midges again, just don't get on the other side of the river and have to make your crossing back in the dark. Kinda funny sometimes how you can lose all your sensibilities, when there's big fish involved.

8/28/2011

Off to my left, I see a slight dimple on the surface of the gin clear, cold water that flows past me, from upriver. Although I can't see him, I know it's a fish, sipping something so small I can't make it out from the twenty five feet that now separates us. Sweat glistens on the back of my neck, from the sun that is peeking through the building clusters of cumulonimbus clouds in an otherwise bluebird New Mexico sky, forming a bead that gathers in size and is pulled by the gravity of the earth, down the hollow of my back. An ever so slight breeze, permeated with the scent of creosote, juniper, and sage passes over me and I look at the tiny Fore and Aft; held between my thumb and forefinger; its small microfibers barley discernible to the naked eye, held there by an invisible piece of tippet, hardly the diameter of a human hair and I automatically begin to strip line from the reel, held in my other. With one false cast, the rod loads and the loop of fly line and leader stretches out, landing the fly about three feet above the growing ring of the dimple, to my target that is no bigger than a pie plate. With the short distance that the fly has to travel, there is no need mend the line, and it floats like a wisp of dust, downward on the current. I again see the tale-tale dimple; a new one this time, and instinctively raise the 8 foot stick of spun graphite and instantly come tight to nineteen inches of chrome and crimson that explodes unmercifully across a fifteen foot expanse of water, faster than you can blink. The little click and pawl screams like a banshee, and minutes later I cradle one of God's most perfect creatures in the crook of my right hand, his aqua green back blending perfectly with the cobbles of the river bottom. The only evidence that separates this life form and a piece of beautiful painted sculpture, is the occasional pulse of his gills, as the highly oxygenated water passes through, reviving him to his former self. With a sudden swish of his broad tail, he disappears from my hand and becomes only an ephemeral memory. That is how I prefer to spend my time away from work, here on the San Juan. If you love to fly fish there are plenty of these moments waiting out here for you, even as you read this. We are experiencing flows right now around 900 cfs, which still makes for very wadeable conditions. The water is in great shape, with crystal clear conditions. For this upcoming week, we should expect to see temperatures in the high 80's to low 90's with chances of thundershowers, each afternoon. Midges are still the dominate food source right now, and although most of the hatches that are occurring around 11:00 and then again at 4:30 or 5:00 are sparse, they are still offering opportunities to catch some fish on small dry patterns. Nymphing is still the most productive way to go throughout most of the day with patterns in sizes 26 to 28 in grey, olive and cream, working best. There is still some good terrestrial fishing available; as well, if you stick to those fish that are holding higher in the water column, or tight against the banks. I have even done pretty well on dry damselfly patterns, with those fish holding in the still waters of the back eddies and side channels. So if you get the chance to get away, the fishing is still very good and it looks like these conditions are probably going to hold for a pretty good while.

Fall

3 FALL

In Season

He crouched his body and eased forward ever so slowly and peered over the edge, now drawing deeper breaths which calmed his rapid breathing and beating heart, caused by the long, strenuous walk and the excitement of being here. Assured that there was nothing in the immediate vicinity, he carefully crept between the two large and protruding boulders just below the rimrock ledge. Taking care to make as little movement as possible, he sat and placed his back against one of the cool rocks that was now in the shade from the crest of the peak and slowly slid the sling of his rifle down his arm and quietly placed it across his lap. Easing out of the straps of his daypack, he drew it toward him and unzipped the top, withdrawing the field glasses and canteen inside. The water, still cold from its filling the night before, seemed to reach his every extremity and he couldn't remember when water ever tasted this good.

Raising the glasses, he began methodically scanning the ridge tops of the adjacent hills, then working across their entire length, until he had reached the bottom of each one. Further to his right he could see the distant peaks now white-topped with snow, and knew that within a few weeks, this very spot where he now sat would soon look the same. The cool wind from the shaded saddle below now rose toward him on the morning thermal lift and brought a slight chill to his face and neck, accentuated by the light sweat he had so carefully tried to avoid by controlling his pace on the hike in. Zipping up the down vest to ward off the chill, he screwed the cap back onto the canteen and placed it into the pack and resumed his glassing at the exact point where he had left off. Taking his time, his eyes soaked up every square inch of the terrain he knew so well; ever diligent, watching for the slightest contrast of brown upon green, the twitch of an ear, or the glint of polished horn in the sunlight that now bathed the facing hillsides.

After what seemed to be a very long time and covering all the panoramic view before him, over and over again, he shouldered the pack and his rifle with the same meticulous care he used in taking them off. Rising ever so slowly to one knee, then fully upright, he stretched his legs that had become stiffened from the sitting and the walk in. Carefully placing his right foot forward, taking every caution possible to plant each boot with its full weight all at once and making sure it was firmly adjusted to the uneven ground beneath, he began picking his way across the skree and shale beneath the ridge, quartering the hillside towards the trail that ran through the head-high aspens that had sprung up in the years after the fire, onwards to the ponderosa pines and into the flats of the saddle below. While still calculating each step and picking out every next footfall, his eyes were yet occasionally drawn toward his final destination, the long draw across this steep, narrow canyon with the quaky leaves of the tall aspens fluttering in the slight wind, shinning in the sun like gold medallions, their branches and trunks like bleached bones in contrast to the surrounding evergreens.

Coming out of the young aspens and entering the flat below, he kept his eyes trained forward, watching for any movement among the little rolling knolls that lay for at least 200 yards ahead, leading to the upcoming hillside. Off to each side, lay narrow drainages that fell off rather quickly, punctuated with scattered oak brush, then large ponderosas, sloping downwards to the corresponding valley floors. At times he could hear the occasional roar from the rush of the stream in the valley, at least half a mile distant, borne on the wind that moved up and across the ridge of the saddle, its intensity rising and falling with each oncoming breeze. Hastening his pace and lowering his profile to limit his exposure over the openness of the trail, he began to push forward, but still taking care not to top out over the knolls too quickly and spook any game that could be hidden on the other side. You could blow an entire hunt by being careless in such situations and the success or failure of a season hung in the balance or either something you did or did not do correctly. Once; years earlier, after glassing the area for a long, long time and assuring himself there was definitely no game in sight, he had carelessly crossed this area and dropped his guard, only to spook a small herd of about a dozen elk. They had exploded in all directions nearly 30 yards in front of him, as he neared the end of the flat, almost at the base of the far hillside. He had been lucky that day, when a few of them had bolted straight up the hill with the last one pausing just at the top, turning full profile for a final look back, giving him just enough time to run the ten steps to the next knoll, throw down his daypack for a rest and make a nice 250 yard shot. Even now he could recall every detail, the big animal crumpling with the report of the shot and tumbling end over end, the entire distance to the bottom of the hill. Sometimes in hunting your luck ran like that; but more often it did not, and he would prefer skill over luck, any day in the woods. So, learning from experience, he tried to always mentally prepare himself for such occasions and gain any edge he could, training himself in every foot of this familiar country he crossed, the location of each game trail, the quietest approaches, the prevailing winds, and the paths that offered the most cover from the watchful eyes of his ever alert quarry.

Nearing the end of this crossing, he could see his intended path up the oncoming hillside, between the big upright boulder and the giant fallen pine, its roots still attached and blackened trunk from the fire years before, its branches now broken and scattered along its length like some great prehistoric skeleton from millions of years past. To the left of his trail was the game trail that came down from the mountain and entered the saddle he had just crossed, the red clay and shale pounded into dust, as fine as talc in the late October sun from the constant traffic of the beasts he sought, making their yearly sojourn to their wintering grounds just as they had for hundreds, maybe thousands of years. This is where he had been some time back, late in the day on the last day of season, with the sun dropping toward the mountains. He had already filled his elk tag days before, but had hoped to take a bear in the few days he had left. Standing quietly and watching the setting sun he was reflecting on what another wonderful hunt this season had been, and began to feel the mixed emotions he always felt as a season drew to a close, thankful for the opportunity to be out in country he loved so much, but with some sadness in seeing it all come to an end, knowing the beauty of the fall would soon be replaced with the snow and harshness of winter. It was always a turning point in the year and his life and made him reflect back on the past. Lost deep in thought, he remembered being startled by a sudden loud crashing in the brush, off to his left. Having already placed his rifle across his back in anticipation for the walk out, he instinctively peeled it off and went into a crouch. Judging by the sound, it was most likely to be an elk and having already filling his tag for the year, he knew that he would not be able to take another, but just the thought of being able to finish off the season with seeing one of these magnificent beasts up close again made him just as excited as his stalk, days earlier. Suddenly though there was a shrill shriek and a rabbit shot past him, nearly running over his feet. While he was pondering the oddity of it all; the noise and the fact he had never seen a rabbit this far back in the timber, and the fact that it had nearly run him over, he caught motion out of the corner of his eye. Headed out the side of the knoll before him was a beautiful black bear, his pelt as dark as night with a wonderful caramel colored snout. He shouldered his rifle and tried to pick him up in the scope, but the bear was moving at a pretty good pace with several large trees between them; and still moving, the bear continued on through the cut of the hill, stopping at the edge where it dropped off to the west, with only the very top of his head and just a bit of his high shoulders showing above the rise that blocked his full silhouette. His heart pounded and in the fading light his mind began racing; as well, on what to do next. The bear was still totally unaware of his presence, but the slightest breeze or movement could change all that. He was only about 50 yards away, but with so little of his body exposed it wouldn't be an easy shot especially with the light fading so fast. He could possibly cut around the rise in front of him and maybe get a broadside shot, but doing so risked spooking or allowing the bear to scent him and he doubted he had that kind of time left, anyway. So, drawing his breath he took his best aim and tried for the top of the shoulder that was scarcely jutting above the rise. As soon as he squeezed off the shot, the bear made a

180 degree turn and headed back the way he had came, at a blazing speed that amazed him. As the bear passed, he fired another shot in his direction, unable to pick up the moving target in his scope, but hoping against all hope that maybe one of the bullets had found their mark. He heard the bear crashing down the drainage, followed by what sounded like him scaling up a tree. With the light almost gone now, he hurried toward the hillside, to where he had fired his last shot. There was still some light snow there that had been protected in the shade of the hill and he immediately began looking for blood and tracks. By now it was growing dark and he scrambled into his daypack for his headlamp, his hands touching familiar objects where he had carefully placed them and could locate what he needed without ever having to actually look into the pack. Darkness falls quickly at this time of year, especially in this steep canyon where he now found himself. He placed the strap of the headlamp around the outside of his cap and flipped on the switch, and gave his eyes a moment to adjust and immediately began; once again, to look for a blood trail or tracks. He saw neither. Back and forth up the small patch of snow he walked, paying close attention to the ground before him. It was a relatively small area covered in snow and he was sure the bear had travelled through it, yet he could not find a single track, much less a drop of blood. Remembering the sound he had thought was probably the bear treeing, he began to walk in the direction he had last seen him travel. Further down the drainage his headlamp focused on the ground hoping to pick up some kind of sign or trail. He didn't remember when it suddenly dawned on him that what he was doing was definitely was not a good idea, but he remembered thinking, "I am at least three miles from the nearest house or road, no one knows that I am out here, and I am looking for a possibly wounded bear in the dark, with only a small headlamp for light." "Time to come to my senses and get out of here and call it a season."

His mind now shifted to another place in time and he remembered someone asking him once, what he thought about when he spent all that time on the river fly-fishing; and after much debate, he admitted that all he thought about out there, was fishing. With hunting it was different, while much of his thoughts out here were totally focused on the hunting, there were many times when he found himself thinking about the beauty of nature and the awe of it all. But, there were also nostalgic moments when he found himself thinking about the events of his life and how they had led him here, or even about the lost loves of his past. Strangely enough, he never worried about the problems that were presently pressing him, in his life or work. Somehow, his brain would just not allow him to burden himself out here with such things. More often than not, he lately found himself thinking about growing older and just not being able to do this anymore, the kind of thoughts that also occupied his mind in the long hours of the nights when he could not sleep. It seemed not so long ago that he covered much more territory back here and sometimes ran across the hills that he now walked more slowly. And there were earlier times when he packed out his elk by himself in two days, when it now took him two or three, with the help he enlisted from friends. He sure didn't enjoy it any less, but it had become harder, and he was beginning to wonder if it would be safer back here with a hunting companion, although he really loved the solitude of hunting alone. He would always stay in the backcountry until last light, walking the entire way back with just a headlamp. Since the fire, he had been forced to hunt deeper into the few places that it had left untouched, so hunting closer to camp was not an option. And over the years more of the burned trees had fallen during the winter storms, creating difficulty in travelling what had always been hard country, to begin with.

Rousing from his daydream, he refocused his attention on the hill before him and he rehearsed in his mind each step and every obstacle that now lay between himself and his final objective. Without even looking, he could see the tight squeeze between the boulder and the large downed pine, the change from dust to pine needles beneath his feet, and the scattered patches of low Gambel oak that dotted the hillside. He could feel the change in temperature from the coolness of the shade under the big ponderosas as he moved up the steeper terrain before him, the burning of the muscles in his legs as they began to work harder to propel him upwards. Nearly halfway up he would turn to his right and make his way around the side of the hill, taking care not to slip on the small gravel of the shale. This would lead him to a small hogback outcrop with a rocky spine that ran down the length of a steep ravine, creating a drop of seven or eight feet into its entrance, and at which there was only one crossing point. Rifle and pack across his back, he would have to pick his way through the cut, then down through the drop and make his way across the upper half of the ravine, at its steepest point. Going down was difficult, but he was always more mentally focused on the much more difficult task of returning, because he had to judge if he was on the correct level of the ravine in order to arrive back at this exact spot and it was usually in the dark when he attempted it. Once he had crossed the ravine he would need to negotiate through a series of small game trails that led across a broad hill, choked with thick brush and a series of large blowdowns left behind by the fire. Successfully managing through this area was harder than it appeared from a distance-chose the wrong way and you could end up at an impassible blockage of blowdowns that would send you backtracking in the noisiest ground of the entire hike in. After passing the blowdowns, he would enter the edge of some half grown aspens; the grove only about twenty yards wide, but running from the top of the mountain all the way to the canyon below.

For the past three years in a row he had jumped a nice mule deer from his bed in this exact same spot, always on his first day back. The buck had never bolted and ran, but rather bounced a few times to gain a little distance between them, then stood staring back; as if reluctant to give up his bed, or acknowledging his understanding that it was elk, not deer, this hunter was after. This past year; during this strange ritual, he marveled at how large and majestic the buck had now become. While he admired its strength and beauty, there seemed to pass between them some sort of mutual feeling of respect, his for the tenacity of this animal to grow to such strength and maturity in such a harsh environment, and the buck's for his earned right as a hunter to share this magnificent country, where they both now stood.

Not too much longer now and he would be at his desired location, just past the small rise ahead that was covered in deep grass and marked by the a huge pine that dwarfed all those surrounding, standing like a beacon at the end of the hill that dropped abruptly into the canyon. At the crest of the hill, he overlooked the tops of the golden aspens and the green coolness of the floor below. The steep slope of the hill was scattered with great blowdowns that appeared as if someone had dropped a giant box of matches and they had fallen criss-crossed down its entire length in no particular pattern whatsoever. The grove of mature aspens ran in a fan shape, broadening as it extended out into the intersection of the bottom of the canyon to his right, its other end coming to a point like a funnel that ended up in a narrow valley about two hundred yards to his left, then continuing up the mountainside. Elk liked to travel through this grove because it was always cooler in here and offered them reasonable cover with a less obstructed path to the water in the valley. This was his favorite spot in the entire wilderness area to hunt. He dropped over the ridge of the hill and stopped three quarters of the distance from where the aspens began, to a familiar area that would allow him to be shielded by the trunks of several overlapping, fallen pines. He sat and laid his gun beside him and let the straps of the pack slide from his shoulders, then began to use the heel of his boot to slowly push away the dried leaves and sticks that had accumulated from last season. The loamy smell of earth beneath the decaying leaves was comforting and familiar and gave him a feeling of closeness with his surroundings. Making sure that the noisy debris was far enough away to allow him to move freely, he began to take all the items he would need for the rest of the afternoon from his pack, so that he would not need to make any unnecessary movements as the day wore on. He placed the cords from his field glasses and his call around his neck, then tucked the one from the call under his vest, so the two would not tangle together. He laid out his gloves and wool cap which he knew he would need later, when his body would begin to cool from the walking, once the sun began to drop. He propped his canteen against the log near his feet where he could still reach it with minimal effort and so it could not tip and roll down the hill. Moving the pack behind him, he leaned into it for a backrest, then stretched his tired legs as he began to feel his body adjust to the contours of the ground beneath. As he began to settle into his now comfortable position his senses heightened; especially to the sounds around him, the chattering of a squirrel in a nearby pine, the flutter from the wings of a Clark's Nutcracker further down in the aspens, and the piercing shrill of a red tail hawk cruising effortlessly down the canyon, then banking on the thermals. He tilted his head back to stretch his back and neck and saw patches of the bluebird sky above, his eyes nearly aching from the blueness of it, scattered throughout with the fluffy white clouds that resembled giant buttermilk biscuits. His vision of it all began to fade to black as his body relaxed and his eyelids slowly began to close, the trees, the sky above, all narrowing down to one single pinpoint, then disappearing as if the entire universe along with all its imperfections had just been sucked into it.

Drifting off into a dream, he saw the small shacks he used to find out in the woods of Appalachia, that had at one time been the homes of the old bachelors he occasionally saw on the front porch of the country store in town, when they would walk the many miles once a month to pick up their Social Security checks. They would sit in their blue overalls and run down brogans, drinking their monthly soda, eating crackers and cheese, or sardines, occasionally making conversation with a few folks from town, but mostly keeping to themselves, silent, savoring the crackers and cheese and sodas, then finishing and without a word to anyone, returning their pop bottles to the store and heading back down the coal dusted railroad tracks toward home. He wondered now if he himself would end up like these men, dropping out of the mainstream of life and the personal relationships it provided, taking solace in nature and the pleasures that the hunting and fishing held for him. He wondered if he was missing the true essence of what life was supposed to be, or if these men had either accidently, or on purpose, had it all figured out and that to live simply and alone held true satisfaction, if you were properly aligned with it.

He could feel himself standing there with the summer heat emanating from the overgrown kudzu, jimson weed, and burdock, staring at the one or two room shanty, their rough hewn yellow poplar lumber, bleached dull white by the weather and sunshine, the rusted sixteen penny nails exposed and pulled by the constant strain of the warping wood, the rusted tin roofs abutted at one end by a chimney of flat stacked limestone, with a blackened hearth that served for both the purpose of heating and cooking. Inside, just the dusty floors and an occasional straight back chair with a hand woven bottom of slippery elm bark, or an iron bed frame with a corn shuck mattress covered in faded blue- striped pillow ticking, the wallpaper usually old newspaper, now peeling after many years of exposure to the elements, and often a chipped porcelain covered washbasin beside a small dust covered mirror and sometimes an occasional straight razor. The only other evidence of past human existence were yards filled with empty pint whiskey bottles and rusted Prince Albert tobacco tins, the regal image of the Prince now partially gone with time and the earth now trying to reclaim both the bottles and the tins, in her own good time.

This was their only mark left on life, dying penniless, often alone, unless they were lucky enough to make it into town before they were struck helpless from their illness, only to die alone in a hospital bed and then buried by the county. This structure fashioned by their own hands, with the back breaking labor of hauling rock, timber, nails, and tin over roadless, rough terrain, their only monument, like the pyramids of ancient pharaohs, left to tell of their existence. This, their harbor from the seas of life's harsh realities, their shelter from the rain, the wind, the sun, the snow, with only uncomfortable beds, and cheap whiskey, and hand rolled cigarettes to bring them any respite from it all.

But; they too, had known the taste of plump, sun-ripened blackberries, the cool taste of clear, sparkling water, as it flowed from cold mountain springs. They had watched the beauty of does with their fawns, the first blooms of the redbuds and dogwoods in spring, the sound of soft summer rains falling on their tin roofs, the quiet stillness of falling darkness, punctuated by only the call of the whip-or-will, or the distant hoot of an owl. They had known the coolness of summer mornings, with dew on the grass, while the fog held back the warmth of the sun and the brilliant whiteness of silent falling snow flakes as big as silver dollars. Yes, all choices come with a price, and it just depends on what you're willing to pay.

9/2/2012

Labor Day Weekend, the last big hurrah of summer and the harbinger of fall. After two fantastic days of fishing, I stood alone, late in the day, on a section of this river that is normally known for its crowds and began to think of how this was a fitting end to yet another summer on the San Juan. A tapestry of lengthening shadows on the canyon walls and the soft sound of the closing of the day, bringing with it a sense of something greater now ending. The finality of another season, past. A certain sadness mingled with that contented feeling that follows a solid day on the water, the contented feeling that follows truth, when you know that you have done your best and been rewarded accordingly. A moment when you are likely to be as close to fulfilled, as at any other such time in life, feeling that "good tired" which means you'll sleep well tonight, satisfied. Hating to see it go, yet knowing its inevitability, the brilliant sunshine of summer replaced with the more benign rays of autumn, the smell of creosote, sage, and summer rain, displaced by that of ripe peaches and the fragrance of roasted chiles. I will surely miss it. As far as how long that quality of fishing that I experienced will hold out, it's hard to say. My experience tells me that the time is near when those big fish I was fooling with that large parachute hopper pattern, will no longer be such willing participants in my game. I'll continue to press the issue for as long as I can; but, in my heart of hearts, I know the peculiarity of the fishing gods and the season just won't allow it. So my advice, dear friends, is to get out there and enjoy it while it lasts--maybe another week, maybe two, maybe longer. Big fish on big flies, it's an opportunity that doesn't come around that often and like fine wine, must be savored. At present, the river flow is near 1,000 cfs, up from 900 a few days ago. This recent increase has seemingly given cause for a lot of moss and debris in the water, much more than one would expect for a modest increase of only 100 cfs. The result has been tougher fishing conditions for the last couple of days, judging from the reports I am hearing. This condition normally subsides with a couple of days and things return to normal rather quickly, at least that's what I hoping to find, when I go back out on Monday. For now it's the usual suspects of assorted midge larva and pupa very early in the morning, then the emerger patterns and small midge dries from about 9:00 a.m. till around 11:00. Remember to check and clean your flies often until we start to see this water clear up. Around 4:30 of so, there has been a resurgence of the midge hatch and it builds to a crescendo right up until dark and can make for some nice dry fly action, if you're willing to stay out a little later. I have been experiencing what I would regard as "epic" fishing on hopper patterns, especially in the transitional zones, between fast and slow currents. My best fishing has been from 3:00 until dark. Those risers earlier in the day on the flat, slow water are a no go, unless you get a little wind that gives you just enough chop to hide that 5X tippet. If you are looking for takers before 3:00, my best advice is to hit the faster water and toss and move, and cover some ground in doing so, or prowl the back channels and target those fish along the sides. It's still important to keep that leader upstream of the fly, even with these larger patterns, so I have been doing a lot of reach casts, then shaking out some fly line up above for a slow, drag free-drift. I've found that it's important to have a laser focus on that fly, especially in the faster, deeper stuff, because a lot of times those big fish will come up out of the depths and roll on the fly and you won't see them until a split second before the take. Those types of fish, if missed, rarely return for a repeat performance. Unfortunately, time only moves one way, and this anomaly won't last nearly long enough. I plan to squeeze out every last minute from these golden opportunities, until I am assured they no longer exist. Fall dates for guide trips are booking up quickly, so if you're planning a trip out, I would call sooner than later.

9/4/2011

There's a lot going on out there. While we eat, sleep; and otherwise conduct our daily lives, the lowly midge of the order Diptera and the taxonomic family Chironomidae is busy doing its thing, as well. This insect is one of the most common and abundant organisms in aquatic habitats and this is especially true for the San Juan River, here in New Mexico. While over ten thousand species of this small insect exist throughout the world, probably the most interesting fact to fly fishermen is that their populations can reach up to four thousand larvae, per square foot. That's a lot of bugs, so it's no wonder that here on the San Juan they are the predominate food of choice for our trout, and thus of such great importance to those of us who pursue fish here. It all begins with the adult female depositing her eggs on the surface of the water (ovipositors), where each egg mass may contain up to three thousand eggs and they sink to the river bottom, then hatch in several days to one week. Once this process takes place they burrow into the mud or attach themselves to vegetation or debris and begin to grow as larvae in an elongated form often referred to as "bloodworms", from their dark red color caused by the hemoglobin in their blood and anyone that has fished here is familiar with the size 18 long shank hook, tied with dark red thread that we use to imitate this part of their lifecycle. Depending on the species, these larva will begin to undergo their metamorphosis into their pupae stage while still in their cases or tubes, and around three days or so later, begin their feeble swim toward the surface aided with a buoyant bubble of gas trapped in their pupal shuck. Of course, imitating these naturals with success will depend on determining the prevalence of their numbers in any particular stage of this metamorphosis and which particular stage the feeding trout are keying on and can range in numerous fly sizes and coloration, but are most often emulated with patterns such as UFO, Silk Midges, Disco Midges, or any other number of flies with patterns that represent slim segmented bodies with a slightly larger thorax area. Due to the fact that midges are not great swimmers, as they struggle to the surface it is at this stage they become most vulnerable to predation to trout by washing into the current and feeding lanes of the fish. Struggling to the top, they usually curl and pulsate, their trapped gas bubbles giving off a silvery sheen. As they move to an inch or so from the surface, their bodies tend to parallel with the surface and straight shanked imitations with flash, cdc, foam or clear beads tend to work best; thus our need for Krystal Flash, Foam Back, Soft Hackle, Scintilla, and other emerger patterns and we can expect to see a lot of dorsal and caudal fins begin to show as the fish begin to porpoise near the surface to eat them. At this point the pupae will attempt to hang suspended in the meniscus, or surface film, as they emerge from their shucks and then fly off to mate within about forty-eight hours. The mating ritual typically takes place in swarms and many of the midges end up on the water, still attached, along with the adult females laying their eggs; causing the midge clusters that we are so fond of here on the San Juan, and imitate with Griffith's Gnats, Fore and Afts, and Dead Chickens, to name a few patterns. So there you have it, these little critters live a short but busy life here on our river, but are an invaluable food source to the trout and a big player in ecosystem that affords us such high numbers of big, catch-able fish. As I type this, they are out there doing their thing right now, and the fishing has been very good, because of it. This next week will; no doubt, be much of the same, with midges being the primary food source. The weather looks nice, with temps dropping down into the low 80's most days and chances of thundershowers in the afternoons. We haven't seen prolific hatches lately, but they have been significant enough to get some heads looking up around 11:00 till 1:00 and then again around 5:00 in the afternoon. If you're out this week remember that these tiny insects exist all the time here and are present at all the varying stages of their life cycle simultaneously within the water system, the challenge will rest with you to figure out which stage the trout prefer at any particular moment in time, but that is just one of the rewarding parts of fly fishing.

9/9/2012

You would think that after years and years of fishing this river week after week, I would tire of it and long to fish some different water, especially when there are so many more options nearly an hour away. Now, I enjoy new water as much as the next guy, and those pretty mountain streams with their beautiful scenery and feisty, hungry fish that attack almost any type of dry fly you throw at them, hold a special place in my heart. I know I should break out of my routine and get up into the mountains and onto some of those streams, before the snow starts to fly, and another high country season slips past me. But, there's something addictive about catching a lot of big fish on water that's as comfortable as your favorite old pair of jeans, that keeps me turning right versus left, out of the driveway, every time I load the fly rod into the car. I know I am a creature of habit, but for me, this river offers enough diversity with its varied runs and glides, deep pools, riffles, and back channels to challenge my angling skills to the point that I can't think of a reason where I would ever consider it mundane. Over the past three weeks, I have caught most of my best fish of the year, all on large dry fly patterns, and in impressive numbers. To walk away from that, requires more intestinal fortitude, than I can seem to muster. I'm talking about thick, strong, long, healthy fish, some of which rivaled my personal best, after fishing this river for many years. Any fisherman would struggle to find reason in leaving here, in search of better water. I'm not naive enough to think that there won't come a time when the "catching" part of all this won't become a bit more challenging, with fewer fish to the net. I'll just keep on making that right turn, until it does. If you plan on coming out this week expect to find the flows around 1,000 to 900 cfs, where it is likely to remain until late October. There are some nice early morning midge hatches that are lasting through 11:00 and have a lot of fish up. Small emerger patterns in grey and black (sizes 26 and 28) and dry patterns, like the Fore and Aft in size 24 will serve you well during these hours. If you go the dry route, plan on 7x tippet, there's lots of fish up, but they're not pushovers. 6x will work fine for your nymph patterns. Once the hatch tapers off, Bling Midges, Monomidges, Zebras, and grey Foam Wings will help fill in the time that follows. As the sunlight becomes less direct I like to switch over to 5x with Hopper and Ant patterns. Around 2:00 pm the wind has been picking up a bit, which is a bonus for fishing with these terrestrials, since it makes the 5x harder for the fish to see. Later in the evening expect to see the midges start to hatch again and you can go back to your morning selections, once you start seeing the fish start to porpoise, or the familiar rings of rises to the adults. I have been sticking to my terrestrial patterns during this time and still finding enough takers to keep me happy, but; no doubt, you would catch more fish on smaller midge patterns, and sticking to 7x tippet for the dries, especially on slower, flatter water. We have been seeing some BWO's lately on the lower river, but the hatches don't seem intense or frequent enough to have the fish interested in them just yet. I'm thinking that we're still a few weeks away from fishing Comparaduns to rising fish, unless the weather cools decidedly and the hatch decides to really kick off. The days are still filled with sunshine and promise--and I can't think of anywhere else I'd rather be right now.

9/11/2011

Well, I knew it was going to happen, just not this soon. I went to bed the other night and it was summer, I woke up the next morning and it was fall. The temperature here has gone from the 90's during the day to the low and mid 70's and we are blessed with some 50 degree nights that are just great for sleeping. I don't think the skies could get any bluer, and the air has taken on that fall feeling of not just cooler, but somehow fresher, cleaner, crisper. I am torn between the feelings to visit my old elk hunting grounds to the north and begin my scouting, or spend my time on the water here and take advantage of this spectacular weather. I guess it's a good problem to have. It looks like we will see more of this beautiful weather for the coming week, with temperatures in the low to mid 70's: flow rates around 800 cfs, and crystal clear water conditions. If you like to fish the San Juan, I just don't know how things could get any better. There is a slight chance of thundershowers for most of the afternoons, but I think we are more likely to see mostly cloud cover, which will bode well for some fantastic dry fly fishing later in the day and lasting into the evening. As an added bonus, most of the mosquitoes are now gone, as well. Fishing has been good, with effective patterns of size 24 to 28 midge patterns, working best. Krystal Flash in black and pupae patterns in olive and grey are working great, and seem most productive when targeting fish in the shallower runs, when fished with little or no weight, with an indicator a foot or so above the fly. The water is cold right now, especially nearer to the dam; where readings of 38 degrees have been recorded, so the midge hatches have been somewhat sparse, but there has been some rising fish around 11:00 till 1:00 and I have been able to take plenty of fish on size 24 Fore and Afts. Around 4:30 or 5:00, the hatch seems to get going well enough to get some heads up again and this has been my go to pattern for that time, too. We are starting to see some increased Baetis activity from the Texas Hole down to the lower river on most days, and the cloud cover that is most likely to happen this week will probably result in some good opportunities to fish size 22 olive bodied Comparaduns and Sparkle Duns to some rising fish. Until the fish get going on the adult Baetis, I would fish these waters with patterns like Fluff Baetis, RS2s, and grey and chocolate Foam Wings. If you can get away this week, now would be the time to spend some quality time on the water-- the mosquitoes are gone, there are no crowds, the weather and the fishing is great; heck they even patched some of Hwy 173 from Aztec to Navajo Dam with real asphalt--what else could a guy or gal that likes to fish, ask for?

9/16/2012

In last week's report I attempted to explain my penchant for fishing my home waters of the San Juan and my proclivity for making them my choice over those located, nearby. Occasionally, as a writer, I sometimes struggle to properly express my feelings and thus convey my thoughts in a proper manner and must defer the work to those far more experienced and talented, in order to do so. Just last night I was reading and came across a piece from the famed fly-fishing writer Roderick Haig-Brown that far better spoke the thoughts on my affinity for fishing familiar waters and more eloquently expressed my reasoning for doing so, that I thought I would be remiss not to share it here. The quote is from his book "A River Never Sleeps" and it goes like this: "And my favorite fishing water would always be the one I know best. For some reason there is more pleasure in catching a fish where you have caught one before and know one ought to be lying than in catching one, more or less blind, from an unknown water. And obviously there must be greater pleasure and merit in learning a new thing about a well-known stream than in learning half a dozen new things in one day about a strange water." Thanks, Roderick--well done, although you glaringly reveal your consummate command of the English language and my lack, thereof. And now we come to that "golden season", when the heat of summer fades, replaced by cool mornings and evenings, and rich, resplendent, fall sunshine. Days on the water, surrounded by the changing colors of the cottonwoods, crisp clean air, and the sound of rushing waters, occasionally punctuated with intonation of geese and ducks, in flight. A grand time to be on the San Juan. Once again I find myself torn between my love for fishing this river, during such a wonderful time of year, and pursuing my second passion, chasing Wapiti in the high country of Colorado. My house, now in disarray from the hunting gear dragged from the closets of last year, speaks volumes for my need to attend, such business. I suspect I will try and equally divide my time between, both. On the days I won't be here, I'll be missing the early morning midge hatches we are seeing, as early as 7:00 am. They are best fished with midge emerger patterns and small dry patterns, right now, like Crystal Flash, Ju-Jus, Scintillas, and Fore and Afts, the emergers in sizes 26 and 28's and the dries in size 24. After the hatch, Red Larva, Mono and Bling Midges, should help bring fish to the net. Late evening brings on another midge hatch here, and the existence of more opportunities for fishing small dry patterns to rising trout. There seems to be more movement in the lower river of Baetis nymphs and the fish in those regions are starting to focus more on the offerings of RS2s, Fluff Baetis, Johnny Flash, and Root Beer patterns. This tells me that the Blue Winged Olive hatches of fall can't be far off, although I suspect it will be in full swing while I am away from the river, in mid October, on my elk hunt. I know I'll try to focus on the sport at hand, but also know that my thoughts will surely wander to the waters of the San Juan and drifting Mayflies and the big trout that like to sip them. Ah!, the trials and tribulations of the sporting life.

9/18/2011

As of September 23rd; 9:04 am Coordinated Universal Time, the sun will cross the celestial equator and begin its trek southward for those of us here in the Northern Hemisphere. This event will mark the autumnal equinox, or the first official day of fall; as we have come to know it, and the days will become shorter, and the nights a little longer, and our temperatures will begin to drop as the sun's intensity wanes. For those of us that spent anytime outside here in New Mexico this past week, we don't need the above information to let us know that fall is on its way, you can already feel it in the air. This coming week's weather out here looks like the quintessential embodiment of the season that people who fish the San Juan love the most--bright, crisp, bluebird days, with highs in the seventies, and lows in the fifties, with little or no chance of rain. I couldn't agree more. The BOR has dropped the river level to around 700 cfs, due to the rains we experienced last week that caused a rise in the Animas' water level and less need for San Juan water, downstream. This level, or a close approximation of it, should stay in place for a while and create some fabulous fishing conditions, combined with the near perfect fall weather. We had a few days this past week, when the rain got a little out of hand and caused a few of the washes to flow and make the water murky for a few hours, but we've returned to crystal clear water conditions and the fishing is very good right now. This river offers some of the most diverse opportunities for a fly fisher, of pretty much any tailwater out there. In the quality water section alone, there are numerous shallow riffles, deep narrow runs (both slow and fast), along with, glassy flats, and countless back eddies, with several side channels and sloughs, thrown in for good measure. Such hydrological diversity lends itself to opportunities to fish some great water with various techniques ranging from swinging big streamers, nymphing small midge patterns, or fishing dry fly patterns, all in a single, walk-able stretch, in a river that is one of the most wade-friendly waters, in the west. Right now, we're experiencing some really good midge hatches around 11:00 and although we aren't seeing huge clumps of midge clusters, there are plenty of occasions to fish for rising fish on small midge dry patterns, and enough fish to keep you busy for hours, doing it. If nymphing is your thing, then there's plenty of that going on, as well. Small patterns like Krystal Flash, Mono Midges, Silk Midges, and Scintillas in sizes 24 to 28, are working well. From Texas Hole and below, there has been some Baetis activity in the afternoon and patterns such as, Fluff Baetis, RS2S, Grey and Chocolate Foam Wings, are taking fish. There doesn't seem to be enough of the adults on the water; just yet, to warrant breaking out the Comparadun patterns, but as the weather cools, I would keep my eyes out for some good hatches, in the coming weeks. If you can make it out to the San Juan this week, you are not going to be disappointed in what Mother Nature has to offer you here. This is, as they say, "As Good As it Gets."

9/25/2011

As much like many things in nature and life; itself, we owe our opportunity to experience the pleasures this world offers, to the cycles she keeps. The hydrological cycle of evaporation, precipitation and runoff is something most of us take for granted, but without it we wouldn't be able to enjoy such rivers as the San Juan. When I am on this river my mind wonders sometimes and I marvel at the crystal clear, pure liquid that is vital for the life form of this great trout fishery. Maybe I might just have too much time on my hands, but just thinking about how this all got here, seems to make this obsession I have for pursuing fish in moving water, all that much more enjoyable. Just to think that the mass of water that now continually flows past my wadered legs and booted feet, began long ago, thousands of miles away in its same form, then transformed itself into an evaporated state, and traveled such a long distance in some nimbostratus cloud until the upward motion of air forced it to ascend the San Juan Mountain range of the Rockies, until the cooler temperatures caused it to form and fall into the crystalline water ice form, we call snow, kinda of blows my mind a little. And then there's the mind boggling feat of its next conversion caused by the thermal energy of the sun, which again returns it to its liquid form as these droplets combine together to form a rivulet, then a small stream, and next a river, as gravity takes over and this liquid flows from miles away in the high mountains of the San Juan watershed, past my feet and all these trout, for this moment and this moment only, on its way back to the sea. Bravo, nature--quite an undertaking. Right now this most abundant compound on the earth's surface is being released from a man-made obstruction in its path, at 500 cubic feet per second, at a temperature of around 38 to 40 degrees in a rich oxygenated and mineral state, creating one of the most prolific fisheries in the world, and I am a happy man, for it. This past week brought us some absolute fantastic weather and some outstanding fishing, as well. I had some incredible days fishing dry flies to big rising fish, and I heard more stories than I can recall in the recent past, of other fishermen having their best fishing, so far this year. As far as what's going on, small midge patterns in grey, like Krystal Flash and Scintillas have been the ticket from Texas Hole on up, and as you head downriver, Baetis patterns like RS2s, Fluff Baetis, and Rootbeers, have been the big producers. There have been some great Baetis hatches, on most days, in the lower river around 1:00 or 2:00 and this past Monday I was able to stretch this hatch out until after 5:00, by tossing a size 22 CDC Comparadun, to fish concentrated in the eddies behind some of the big boulders and structures, that seemed to just keep pumping out little olive Mayflies. It's been a little busier than usual on the river lately, and I don't know why I am always surprised to find that I'm not the only one who has discovered that this time of year, with the fish on the feed, and the perfect weather, and the absence of mosquitoes, is an awesome time to fish the San Juan. However, given the abundance in the number of fish here, you don't need a lot of water to still catch a lot of trout on this river; and really, there's so much fishable water, I never feel like I can't get a little solitude, if I'm willing to walk a little bit. If that's your thing, there's plenty of nice fish in the 14 to 16 inch range, left over from a recent stocking, just below the Crusher Hole and unlike their picky relatives in the upper Quality Water, they're pretty eager to come to larger flies-- a size 18 Pheasant Tail, fished under a bright egg pattern, will get the job done. It looks like we have several weeks of this great weather left, so now's the time to start planning your trip here and enjoy some of the beautiful fall sunshine, that helps make all this wonderful cycle of water and life, so enjoyable to all us fishermen.

9/30/2012

There's a bridge that crosses the river here in town and no matter how many times you cross it, your eyes are invariably drawn to the water that runs beneath. Unless you're a fisherman, you'll most likely see only water flowing under a bridge. For me, and others that fish, we probably tend to gaze a little longer, pensively tracing its course, taking note of both the shallowness and deepness of it, the way the current makes its broad curve to the outside bank, creating the thalweg that holds a foam line to the middle of the run. We'll see the cobbled bottom of the shallows, and imagine the larger rocks that exist beyond the surface, where we cannot see. And always we'll try and form those mental pictures of those subaqueous creatures, submerged beyond our field of vision, from this perch which we must pass over, at the required 35 mile per hour speed limit. It's a habit no true fisherman can break, dissecting the water, conceptualizing where; or where not, fish may lie, and it continually stirs in us thoughts of other sections of the river's reaches and how we should like to be there at that precise moment. Such an inescapable conundrum has only one remedy and that is to go fish. That is what I am advocating right now and you couldn't pick a better time to visit the San Juan, than the present. With flows of 800 cfs, outstanding fall weather, the yellowing leaves of the cottonwoods, and the matching blooms of the surrounding chamisa, it's a wonderful place to be. I should also mention that the fishing is great. Normally, I'm not a proponent of early morning fishing here, as this river tends to lend itself more towards banker's hours during most parts of the year; however, if you snooze right now, you're gonna lose--lose out on an early morning midge hatch that can start your day out right with some great dry fly fishing with small midge adult patterns. It's worth dragging your butt out of bed a few hours earlier for, and technically, making the most out of your fishing day, since the days are getting shorter anyway, and you can't fish as late into the evening as you did only a month ago. Below the Texas Hole to Last Chance, Baetis nymphs such as Fluff Baetis, Root Beers, Chocolate and Grey Foam Wings, and RS2s, seem to be the ticket. These nymphs seem to be getting more active in anticipation of the later autumn hatches, and the fish are on to them. There have been some sporadic BWO hatches throughout the day on the lower river, some occurring as late as 4:00 pm. At best, they're unpredictable, from a timing perspective, but I wouldn't leave the parking lot without a few comparaduns in my box, size 22 and 20. Once you see the adults on the water, tie one of these on and you're in for at least about 45 minutes to an hour of dry fly nirvana. I fished a hopper pattern most of the day this past Monday with mixed results, some takers, but not a lot. However, I'm not fully convinced that the days of the hopper are over just yet, since my experimental control conditions became somewhat skewed by the weather that seemed to change every five minutes from rain and wind, to sunshine and calm, then back again, repeatedly throughout the day. I plan to give it another shot, just to be sure of the results. I have been hearing some good reports on the streamer fishing-- bunny leeches and woolly buggers in olive, brown and black, and since I rate this method of taking fish a close second to my penchant for the dry fly, I plan to swing a few in the coming days, as well. The fish that I have been catching have been heavy and healthy, and my theory is that the higher flows we have been seeing throughout the summer have served them well, by churning up a lot of protein to bulk up on. There are also a lot of little guys out there right now, due to numerous stockings of thousands of fish that were originally destined for other New Mexico waters, but averted to the San Juan because of low water conditions in those other streams. The DOW biologist assures me that this river can support them and I have no reason to doubt him. While they can be considered pesky at times (depending on where you fish), I think the end benefit will justify the slight inconvenience you may incur in the short term and given the traditional growth rate of San Juan fish, we will likely see some phenomenal fishing in the next few years here. Every day is a new day for this river, and just when you think you've seen it all, along comes a new Mona Lisa, or you find Jimmy Hoffa under some guy's driveway in Michigan, life imitating art, I love the challenge.

10/2/2011

I had heard it in the shop all week from a lot of different people, "the best fishing of the year this far", "the river is on fire right now", " the fishing was unbelievable today". Well, I have been around enough fly shops in my life to know that you have to take such claims with a grain of salt, and that terms like "the best fishing of the year" and "unbelievable fishing", are all relative terms. But, I had heard it enough last week to start me thinking that there just might be something to this, or either that it was some kind of big fly fishing conspiracy, designed to get me to fish more, so I decided to check it out for myself. Well, I'm here to tell you that sometimes it pays off to listen to some of the claims you may hear in those fly shops, because I went out Monday and Tuesday and had one of those "best fishing days of the year this far", for myself. For those who golf or fly fish; for that matter, you know that if you play enough, you'll have one of those days where the club meets the sweet spot on the ball with every swing, and you get that lucky bounce every time, and the ball falls into the cup on each putt, even if you read the lie wrong. Sure it helps, if all the conditions are right and the wind and all the elements are stacked in your favor, but it's a beautiful thing when everything just seems to fall into place, and you can do no wrong. Fly fishing writer Nick Lyons calls it "playing tennis with the net down", a term he borrowed from the poet Robert Frost, and while I probably wouldn't enjoy this sport quite as much, if every time I fished, it was that easy, I've spent enough time on the other end of this spectrum to appreciate it, when it comes. So, what makes it so much easier right now, than other times? Well, if I really had the answer to that, I could sell it and probably wouldn't have to work anymore. However, I do have a few theories. I was recently speaking with a Fish and Game Biologist here, and we were discussing the fact that some lament the fact that this river doesn't have many of the "timed" hatches of bigger bugs like stone flies, green drakes, caddis, etc. that other river are famous for, and it upsets them that they have to fish these tiny midge patterns, all the time. But I see the glass half full. To me it's a bonus that midges are the primary food source of these San Juan fish for several reasons. For one, I think it's great that I don't have to wait for the "right week" and all the stars to align just right, for the fishing to be good, and I like the fact that the size of our bugs are smaller, forcing the fish to eat more of them, to get their sufficient nutrition. I'll take consistency over size any day, and these little buggers are out there 365 days a year. Right now the conditions are just right for some great midge hatches that are lasting all day long and in the lower river the Baetis are really beginning to come off on a regular basis between the hours of 2:00 and 4:00. If that's not enough reason to get your attention, there was a stocking this week of 1,800+ fish in the range of 14 to 15 inches, with a few around 20 inches, from the Texas Hole on down in the Quality Water Section and the Lower Section around Pump House Run is still fishing great, with increased numbers of fish from a recent stocking, there. The flow right now has gone up just a bit to 746 cfs, due to a drop in the Animas, and the weather looks to be a little cooler next week, with a chance of thundershowers on most evenings and this may result in a drop in the release level from Navajo Dam, if there is a substantial rise in the Animas. Not to worry: however, it's not going to be anything dramatic enough to affect the quality of the fishing. If anything, these upcoming overcast days, will just make it better, if that is possible right now.

10/7//2012

A friend and I once spent a summer in the small town of Cooper Landing on Alaska's Kenai Peninsula. Our purpose for being there was to fish, and fish we did. Summertime in the Land Of the Midnight Sun, lends itself to a lot of fishing opportunities, because; as the title suggests, you never really experience darkness during the course of a normal day. While this anomaly could be viewed as a boon for those who really love the outdoors, it can also lead to some negative consequences for those with an unbridled enthusiasm to fly-fish, in that you could literally-- fish yourself to death. On one particular day during one of the salmon runs, we both went on a "fishing binge" that started on the Kenai River, then on to Russian,

Kasilof, Ninilchick, Anchor, and might have even included Quartz Creek. At some point towards the end this "fishathon", my friend found me lying on the cobbled banks of the Kasilof, exhausted, finally trying to take a little streamside nap, using a rather large rock as a pillow. It was at that precise time that he asked me, if I realized that we had been fishing for the past 26 hours; and honestly, I hadn't really bothered to notice. Now, part of that was drive time between rivers; but not much, the entire distance from our starting point to the last river was only two hours, and all the others were along the way. I'm not suggesting you try anything as extreme as this in the upcoming weeks, or anytime; for that matter, but this beautiful fall weather isn't going to last forever and you don't want to find yourself sitting next to the fire when the snow is flying in December, wishing you had taken advantage of it while you had the chance. And as someone once said: "there aren't any fish rising in the graveyard", thus my advice is to get out, if you can. The fishing, as well as the "catching" part of the sport, is hard to beat on the San Juan right now. We have been seeing midges coming off for the biggest part of the day and my old favorite, the Fore and Aft seems to be the ticket for the risers. From the Upper Flats through the lower river, there have been some short, but sweet, BWO hatches on most days and a CDC Olive Comparadun in size 22 works great when the fish key in on these adult Baetis. If you are nymph fishing in any of these areas, I would have some Chocolate Foam Wings, RS2s, and Fluff Baetis patterns. Above the Texas Hole, you are going to need some Red and Cream Larva, UFOs in Grey and Brown, and the usual assortment of midge emerger patterns, when you start seeing those porposing riseforms. I had a good day last Monday in the upper river, fishing a weighted Olive Woolly Bugger and have heard some good reports on the same pattern in Brown, as well. If you like fishing streamers, now's the time--I kept the same fly on all day long on Monday and caught fish (I did switch to a Black Wooly Bugger for about an hour) but my catch rate went down, and I went back to the Olive. I like swinging these flies with an upstream presentation in faster water and staying tight to the line through the drift, fishing it all the way through the run, with a slow retrieve at the end. According to the BOR, the river flow will be dropped to 650 cfs on Tuesday at 8:00 am. I don't look for this to affect the fishing any and I personally prefer fishing it at that level because it opens up more water that I can wade and makes the fish a little easier to spot for sight fishing. So you've got a lot of options, depending on whatever method you may choose, they're all catching fish right now. Get out if you can, the mornings and evenings are a bit chilly so bring a jacket that you can peel off during the warmer part of the day. We've had some wind for the past few days, but the rest of the week looks like that will die down considerably and we should have lots of sunshine with average daytime highs around 70 degrees.

10/9/2011

"There is a bit of moving water, a few trout rising, and you. That's where all value begins in fly fishing." Those are the words of Nick Lyons, a fly fishing writer that I am beginning to appreciate more and more, each time I read his work. That statement really speaks to me and simplifies and crystallizes the reason I have spent countless hours driving all night with no sleep, eating food from gas station microwaves, and drinking bad coffee to reach one destination or another, that promised to be the next new "hot spot." It explains to me why I have slept in the dirt, or on the snow, and endured all types of extreme weather, just to have a few hours to spend on such moving water. And it gives me a better understanding why I have expended much so blood and treasure on the latest new space age technology gadget or fly rod, which is supposed to give me the edge over the next fish I encounter. It provides reason for the times I have strapped on a 50 lb. backpack, and disappeared into the wilderness, braving large animals that could maim; or worse, kill me, pushing myself to my physical limits and exertion, just to reach some place that would afford me another opportunity to catch fish that may; or may not even exist, once I got there. In the end it always seemed to boil down to a bit of moving water, a few rising trout, and me. Today, I am a little older; and hopefully a little wiser, and I don't push the envelope quite as hard now; but even now, when I have surrounded myself with the beautiful scenery and wonders of nature, I find myself tuning out those distant snow covered peaks, or fields of wildflowers, to focus on that one rising fish before me and concentrate wholly on how I will present my next cast and make that perfect drift, set the hook at just the right moment, and become connected to--this one fish, this only fish, that exists in my here and now.

Well, despite some not so friendly weather, there were plenty of those moments available on the San Juan, this past week. We had some wind and rain and some unseasonably cold weather, but the fishing was wonderful. There have been some great hatches of both midges and baetis, all over the river, lasting for hours on end, and the fish are taking full advantage of the abundance of insects, and you can find trout rising to one or the other at almost any hour of the day. And I mean big healthy trout. Lots of them. Those blue-winged-olives seem to like bad weather, and the nastier it gets, the more prolific the hatch. I have seen them in small numbers; recently, as early as 11:00 and then really get going, thick, around 1:00, and I am still seeing them in noticeable amounts, as late as 6:00. They are showing up, not just in those predictable places like Baetis Bend, but all the way up river, into the Upper Flats, region. In the early and later hours when the Baetis are not on the water, the midges have been able to fill the gaps, and have a lot of heads, looking up. Recent flow reductions to the mid 500 cfs range have produced some great opportunities for sight fishing, allowing you to pick out and work the individual fish of your choosing.

Beginning Monday, Oct 10th the BOR will begin a $300,000 restoration project on the river. The first phase will address the Rex Smith Wash, and the silting problem associated with that area. Due to work and heavy equipment in that area, the trail that leads to upper flats, from the Texas Hole parking lot will be inaccessible during this time. To access that area, you will either have to wade upriver, or reach it from the upper BOR parking lot. The next phase will begin sometime in November, and will consist of habitat improvement and the redirection of more water to the Braids area, which will create more fishable water, there. This work will last through November and most of December, and that area of the river will be closed to fishing, during that time. The entire project is expected to be completed on Jan. 8th. There have been rumors that the flows may be adjusted down to 250cfs, during the time the Braids work is being done, but I haven't seen anything official to support this yet. We'll investigate further, and get back to you here, either way. If so, the river is still fishable at 250cfs, so not to worry.

10/13/2011

Outside a full moon rises to the east. A hunter's moon, large and orange; at first, then rising faster and becoming a bright white orb that casts an almost eerie glow over the sandstone cliffs and pinions that dot the distant landscapes. A moon that is calling me to the hunt. Soon the sound of bugling elk will fill the air and this moon will help to light my path back to camp in the long late hours after their pursuit. I will apologize in advance for the brevity of this report; but hopefully what is lost in brevity will be made up for in substance. I am leaving for a few days to Colorado to spend some time in the mountains to chase the elk. I leave the river with mixed emotions. The fishing right now is the best it has been all year. The weather is beautiful with temperatures in the seventies, the cottonwoods are beginning to turn a brilliant yellow, and the air has a that fall crispness to it; that anyone that has spent any time out west in the fall, has come to love. But there are a few last minute details to wrap up before I head north, so I need to impart a little info to those that are lucky enough to be here in the coming week. You are in for a treat. The river is flowing at around 550 cfs with crystal clear water conditions. There are lots of fish available from the recent stocking, especially in the Texas Hole Area. It's pretty much midges in smaller sizes during the early morning hours in olive and grey, with plenty of opportunities for fishing small dry patterns like the Fore And Aft. Around 12:00 to 1:00 start looking or the emergence of Baetis, and the chance to tie on a size 22 or 20 Comparadun, and have some of the best dry fly fishing of the year. If you're fishing the lower flats and below, I would definitely drift some Grey Foam Wings, RS2's and Fluff Baetis, until you start seeing fish take the adults. This may take a while—observe the fish and see what they are doing—I have watched these hatches start for the past few weeks and these fish will let a lot of drifting blue wing olive adults pass by for quite a long time, and sip midges right next to them, before they begin to key in on these bugs. But, once they start, it's on. The entire river is fishing great right now, so you can't go wrong from Cable Hole to Last Chance. It's hard to leave, but I love to hunt about as well as I love to fish, so there you go.

10/14/2012

You bend over, hands on your knees and stare down numbly, mindlessly, at the tops of your boots now covered in the fine dust from the trail. You shrug your shoulders to shift the weight of your pack a little higher onto your back and draw big lungfuls, deep down diaphragm gasps, of cool, clear mountain air as you turn your head up to face the trail, a bead of sweat rolls down and drips from the end of your nose. It's only about 500 yards more to the top of the first of many more rises and you see the younger guys already standing at the top and you wonder if you can still do this. Unless you're the lead dog, the view never changes. No Country For Old Men. Humping out an elk quarter in this terrain is hard work, but when you're finally back in camp, the music never sounds sweeter ,the beer never tastes better, the wind and the sun both cooling and drying your sweat soaked clothes, somehow make you feel more alive today. How many miles is it? All of us hunt it, but none of us really knows for sure. Two? two and a half?, three? Probably more like two as the crow flies, but it sure seems like a lot more with this heavy pack. If you're not in shape by the time season begins, you sure will be by the time it ends, or else they'll find your emaciated carcass lying somewhere along his trail. Just a couple more seconds to catch your breath, you think about this year's past surgeries and wonder if all the stitches, mesh, and metal parts hammered into bone, are all going to hold, then rise, arch your back to stretch your aching muscles, and push on. I love to hunt, but it's days like that from last week that really make me appreciate fly fishing. And what a wonderful time to be in Northern New Mexico on the San Juan River, it is. Beautiful, bright fall days in the mid 70s, the yellowing leaves of the cottonwoods along the river for a backdrop, cool, crisp morning air, and fish--lots of them. Yeah, I've heard the complaints that there's a lot of small fish out there right now and it's true. NM Game and Fish has stocked somewhere around 235,000 fish in the San Juan so far this year (it's a bad time to be a bug on the river), due to low water conditions elsewhere around the state, and most of them have been in the 7 inch or smaller range but there's still plenty of the big guys out there and you can avoid the little stockers, if you're willing to walk a bit. If you're looking for bigger quarry, my advice is to stick to the deeper faster runs, away from where a stocking truck can access. It's still the same repertoire of flies, small midge patterns, especially in the upper river above Texas Hole and a mix of midges and baetis patterns below. We're still seeing decent midge hatches in the mornings and later in the evenings, so dry fly opportunities still exist, just keep the offerings small, since there aren't a lot of big clusters out there. The baetis hatches are infrequent and short in duration, but it's worth carrying a few comparaduns in size 22 in your box, especially if you're fishing the lower river. During the down time before or between hatches, midge pupa and larva patterns in brown, grey, cream, and red, should keep you into fish. I still like weighted streamers in olive and brown, especially if you are targeting bigger fish and have had my best success sticking to the transitional water between faster and slower currents. You probably won't rack up a lot of numbers fishing this way, but the ones you do catch will be memorable. The flow is around 650 cfs and will probably stay around that level for a while. There's a substantial amount of didymo out there, so check and clean you flies often. Due to the great weather, it's a bit busy out there, but still a far cry from the crowds of years past and there's still plenty of open water and lots of fish to catch. Either way, it beats punishing your body by carrying a backbreaking pack up and down steep mountain ranges.

10/21/2012

Like the cat said, when the rocking chair went over his tail, "It won't be long now." We've enjoyed unprecedented fall weather so far, and the cottonwoods are now at their peak with autumn foliage, the temperatures have been in the low 70's for weeks, with lots of blue sky and sunshine, it's hard to imagine how it could have been any nicer. Unfortunately, it can't last forever. Mother Nature is going to do her thing in good time, and this week looks like it will be a turning point as our seasonal changes begin to take place. Judging from the weather reports, it appears that we may have some precipitation on Wednesday and the temps will dip to the 40's for the day, then back into the 50's for the remainder of the week--I doubt we'll see the 70's again this year. I know I'll have to accept it, but I don't necessarily have to like it any more, for that matter.

The fishing for the month of October has been great, and while the weather may be headed for a bit of a change, I don't think we are likely to see a difference in the quality of our angling for a while. The early morning bite has been a little slow, as the temperatures have dropped, but the afternoons have sure made up for it recently. There have been some really good midge hatches around 10:30 or 11:00 a.m., with lots of fish feeding with reckless abandon on the usual small midge patterns, and even opportunities to fish some larger midge cluster patterns, when they really get going. Just as this hatch starts to taper off, the baetis start up and a switch to RS2's, Fluff Baetis, and Grey and Chocolate Foam Wings, will get you into fish. I don't know why, but it always seems to me that it takes a little while before these fish start to key in on the adult BWOs. I've watched as numerous BWOs floated right over the noses of fish, for the first 15 minutes or so, as the hatch begins, and they don't even so much as get a look. I know that they are much more visible than the tiny midges that these fish have been eating, and they seem like easy pickin's to me, but until they pass by in numbers and duration, they don't really become a target for San Juan trout. Then like magic, all the fish seem to rise in unison and that's all they seem to want to eat. Watch for these little sailboats to appear around 1:00 p.m. and keep your eyes on how the fish react to them. Once you see these adults start to disappear to fish, tie on a size 20 or 22 Comparadun pattern, and have at it, for hours. My recipe for a great day of fishing right now would be to target the upper river in the morning, nymphing with midge patterns, then switch to a midge dry, like the Fore and Aft, once you start seeing rises to the adult midges. Fish out the rest of the morning with dries until the hatch starts to taper off, then hightail it downriver and start looking for the baetis hatch. If the adults aren't on the water just yet, nymph with baetis patterns, until you start to see them appear and the fish start to key on them, tie on a comparadun and fish that until it's over, then head home, have your favorite cocktail, and repeat the following day, if necessary. The work has begun on the Rex Smith Wash, to address the silting problem there, but has not interfered with the fishing in that area, outside of blocking the entrance to the trail to the upper river from the Texas Hole parking lot. The work on the Braids Area is set to begin around the first of November and the flow is expected to drop to 250 cfs to facilitate that project. During this time the Braids area will be closed to fishing, but the rest of the river will fish just fine, and you will still be able to drift the river in a boat at the 250 flow.

10/23/2012

The end of this weekend marks a change for this town. After today, the crowds move out, our restaurant closes for the season, the snowbirds pack their RVs and head for a warmer climate and this little section of Northern N.M. gets a lot quieter. There's football and the World Series on t.v., the cottonwoods lose their yellow fall brilliance and begin to fade to brown, the morning and evening air take on a sharper chill, and the daylight hours become noticeably shorter. The ducks and geese are on the move, a harbinger of another season soon to follow. In a few weeks or so, we're likely to see our first sign of snow and we'll settle into a pace that will be more appropriate for when the sidewalks roll up around 7:00 p.m. here. As they say down in Texas--"It's fixin' to be winter soon." However, this little shoulder season has still got a little life left in it, and there's still some good weather ahead of us, and despite the shorter days, lots of good fishing. The blue winged olives are starting to show up in numbers and on lots of days, especially early in the week, you can have entire stretches of the river to yourself, casting dry flies to rising trout. We fish all winter here, except in the worst of weather, but the next few weeks while the weather is still nice and the crowds are gone, are especially favored by the locals. There are still midge hatches in the later morning hours and you can find trout sipping them in lots of places sometimes until around noon. My favorite way to fish this river right now is to go upriver in the morning and target those guys with midge patterns until the hatch tapers off, then head downriver (anywhere between Upper Flats and Last Chance) by 1:00 or 1:30 and get positioned for the BWOs. Generally speaking, the first appearance of a few of these bugs on the water does not warrant much excitement by the fish. Most times, it takes a good 30 minutes or so of a sustained hatch of these BWOs, before you start to see consistent rises. The little fish tend to be the first to key in on the adults and you can distinguish them from the bigger ones by their tale-tale splashy rises, but they are always a sign for what is to follow. As the hatch picks up in intensity and duration, you will begin to see the larger fish start to join the fray. You can catch some fish by blind casting a fly onto the water during this time and hoping that it drifts into the feeding lane of an unsuspecting fish, but I think your chances will greatly improve if you take a little time and get a better picture of what's actually going on around you. First, I like to look for those fish that are consistently feeding and holding in one particular spot. You'll usually notice a rhythm that they will fall into which seems more of a timing thing than holding near the top trying to eat every bug that passes their way. It helps tremendously to time your cast so that your fly passes your fish around the time he is due to rise. Try to position yourself above and to the side of the fish you've chosen and make your cast across and slightly downstream to the lie of the fish. I like to put my fly three feet or so above the fish and a foot or two past them and then drag the fly back into the feeding lane by raising the rod tip and moving the fly where I want it. Once you've got it where you want it, immediately drop the rod tip and follow the fly like a laser. I think you'll find that the initial movement of the fly will help your eyes key in on your imitation and help you to pick it out from all the naturals on the water, and by positioning yourself above and to the side of the fish, you'll be able to keep your leader, line, and tippet, out of the view of the fish. You can shake out a little loose line with the rod tip once you drop it, if it's a particularly tricky drift; but most times, the three feet it has to travel won't require it and it allows you to keep a lot of slack off the water between you and the fish, creating a faster, easier connection between rod and fish when he rises to the fly. At this point, all it usually takes is a slight lift of the rod tip to make a good hook set, since you have a pretty direct nexus between you and the fish. As far as don'ts--don't try to cast over or upstream at these risers, unless you can keep your leader (and I mean leader--forget about fly line) well to the side and out of view of the fish. No self-respecting San Juan trout is gonna fall for any monofilament or fluorocarbon drifting over his head. Finally, I like CDC comparaduns as BWO imitations for these fish and the fish seem to like them and it's something I can see. Size 22 is about right for what's out there right now and 6x tippet will work just fine, especially if you keep it above the fish and the fly is the first thing they see. That's about my 2 cents for fishing dries in a BWO hatch and if it sounds too technical, it's really not, and I guarantee you it's a lot more fun than it sounds like here. Hope you can get out and enjoy the last of this wonderful fall weather and experience some of this great fishing that goes along with it.

10/28/2012

"The reports of my death have been greatly exaggerated"--Mark Twain. If the San Juan River could talk, it would probably use this Twain quote right now. In the past few days I have heard several variations of the rumor that the entire quality water section will be closed to fishing beginning November 1st. and there is panic in the streets in the little town of Navajo Dam, New Mexico. Nothing could be any farther from the truth. Twain also said, "It ain't what you don't know that gets you into trouble. It's what you know for sure that just ain't so.", and that quote too, is apropos of the situation. To set the record straight, the real truth is that the "Braids" section of the river (which encompasses the area just below the Kiddie Hole to just above the Middle Flats/Sand Hole area) will be closed to fishing from Nov. 1st till sometime around Dec. 15th, to facilitate stream improvement work, in that area. The flow rate for the river may be dropped to 250 cfs during this time, but more than likely it will be around 350 cfs, according to reliable sources. The good news is that this still leaves a lot of river to fish during this time; and that once the work is finished, we'll have a whole new section with improved fish habitat, to explore. And yes, the river will fish just fine during the lower flows, and you'll still be able to float a drift boat from the Texas Hole down to Crusher Hole without getting out and dragging the boat over low spots. The worst you can expect on this float is skimming a little gravel bottom, in a spot or two, but nothing that is going to hurt or damage a drift boat. The fish may be a little more concentrated in spots that you are currently unaccustomed to, but with a little old fashioned scouting work, with such low and clear water conditions, they won't be too hard to find. For me, I see it as an opportunity to fish some different water with more concentrated numbers of fish rising to the great hatches we have been experiencing, in easier sight fishing conditions, and as Doc Holliday would say, "That's just my game." So don't worry, all those fish that aren't in that closed area, are not going magically disappear and suddenly get lockjaw. Keep fishing those small grey, black, and olive midge pupae patterns in the earlier hours until the good midge hatches start around 10:30 or so, then switch to small midge dry patterns, when you start to see the risers. Keep fishing those midge dry patterns until that hatch tapers off, then head down river somewhere between the lower Texas Hole to the bait water and start fishing RS2s foam wing and CDC patterns, until the Baetis hatch gets going, then switch up to CDC Comparaduns in size 22 to 20. You can expect more great weather, with highs around 60 degrees for most of the week, with a chance of showers on Wednesday, and a possible shower and maybe just a little snow and lower temps on Saturday, but overall a great week for fishing the San Juan. The clouds and lower temps on Wednesday and Saturday could bring on even better conditions for the great Baetis hatches we have been experiencing lately, just bring some rain gear and warm clothing and you could experience some epic dry fly fishing on BWO patterns.

10/30/2012

Occasionally, there's a bit of truth in such phrases as: " One day we'll look back on this and laugh." I'll agree that there have been a few such occasions where my unbridled passion for fly fishing has led me into such situations where the phrase has been most apropos, and I'm thankful that either age, or the supposed wisdom that comes with it, seems far less likely to lead me down that path of questionable behavior. When I was a bit younger, and perhaps a bit more foolish, I spent a summer with my best friend and fishing partner, camping along Alaska's Kenai River, in pursuit of salmon and the trophy size rainbows that call that area home. We had a crude little camp hacked out in the bush that was long on such things as privacy and backwoods ambiance, but somewhat short on the comforts most people would associate with home. Such conditions, especially when removed from the need to impress the opposite sex, often lead young men to lower the bar on what would be considered normal hygienic practices, but eventually there comes the need, either through guilt or consideration for one's tentmate, for a good old fashioned bath. When the time came, we developed a most efficient ritual, which in its simplest terms, involved only a bar of soap and the glacial runoff of the Kenai River. To begin with, we picked an early hour that was devoid of the prying eyes of fellow fisherman in driftboats and gawking, picture taking tourists in rubber rafts from the nearby Kenai Princess Lodge. The next step was to wade out to the limit considered the Rubicon of the male anatomy, wearing nothing but a smile. Then came just enough splashing of icy water that one's upper torso and head could stand, followed by a thorough soaping of all parts considered. And at last, the dénouement, which involved a deep breath and a quick dunk of the entire body, and Hallelujah! If I remember correctly, there was no need for coffee on those mornings. A lot of time has passed since then and apparently I've grown a little softer over the years, but maybe that experience has made the comfort of my warm bed and access to a hot shower, just a little more enjoyable, and necessary, now. I consider myself blessed, to be able to roll out of the sack, hit the button on the coffee maker and be on the water of one the nation's best trout streams in less than 30 minutes, if I really push myself. With the onset of daylight savings time; thus shorter days, great weather, the disappearance of summer crowds, and fantastic fishing conditions; now more than ever, I feel the need to set the alarm a little earlier and take advantage of all this river has to offer, before the snow starts to fly. Right now there's a great morning midge hatch that I don't want to miss, with the opportunity to toss small dry imitations to any number of rising fish. Then, I'll break one of my cardinal rules of fly fishing and force myself to leave rising fish to head downriver and find others, sipping the BWOs that are showing up around 1:00 or 1:30. At least I can justify this to myself by the fact I know I'll find rising fish, I'm fishing different water, and the flies are a little bigger and easier to see. If you're a nymph fisher, there are ample opportunities; as well, with small midge larva, pupa, and emerger patterns, especially above the Texas Hole. Below Texas Hole, concentrate more on Baetis patterns, like grey and chocolate Foam Wings, olive RS2s, and Fluff Baetis imitations. I would also be remiss to leave out the streamer aficionados here, as those tactics have been effective, as well. As a matter of fact, I'll probably head out Monday and swing Olive conehead patterns until it's too dark and cold to fish anymore, because I like the addictive, heavy tug that goes along with that type of fishing. Tuesday will be devoted to the dry fly only method. Whatever your choice, it's hard to argue with the outcome these days, as the river is fishing great. If you do come out, just don't bother to look for that guy sans clothing with a bar of soap in hand, I assure you those days are over.

11/4/2012

Although the calendar doesn't quite back me up on this, I'm going to go ahead and declare that it is winter. For me, anytime the temperature gets around 20 degrees at night and the high for the day is only in the low 40's, it winter. And that white stuff I saw blowing around in the wind yesterday, only adds credence, to my theory. This coming week looks like we will see some rain and snow on Monday and Tuesday with highs in the 40's, then a bit warmer from Wednesday through Friday with some sunshine, then some more rain and possible snow on Saturday and Sunday. But fishing when the temperatures are in the 40's, can still be comfortable out here, and anytime you're not pausing to knock the ice out of your guides after every cast, is considered tolerable by my standards, especially when the fishing is as good as it has been recently. So my advice right now is to layer up a bit and get out there between 10:00 a.m. and 3:00 p.m., before it really, truly, is winter. To quote the writer Patrick J. MacManus, "The two best times to fish is when it's raining and when it ain't." As far as conditions go, the flow rate right now is 331 cfs and will most likely stay around that level, into mid- December, until the work on the Braids area is finished. The water is still crystal clear, except on some days between Monday through Thursday, when the heavy equipment work is stirring up some debris that carries downriver from the Braids area. There is still some great fishing to be had in both the lower and upper river right now and you'll just have to play the lower river on a day to day and hour by hour basis for water clarity, until the work is finished. If it does get too cloudy down there, there is still plenty of fishable water above the work, and no work is being performed Friday through Sunday, so those days are going to fish just fine from the Texas Hole through the lower river. Just remember, if you wish to access any of the water above the work zone, you will need to do so from the BOR parking area. The baetis hatches are still hanging in there strong and have been starting around 1:00 p.m. each day. Olive bodied Comparaduns with dark grey wings in sizes 22 and 20 have been the ticket, and dark olive, grey, and black midge patterns in sizes 24 to 28, when the BWO's are not active. There have been some good midge hatches, as well, and plenty of opportunities to fish some midge dry patterns. From the looks of the weather, it could be a great week for some awesome dry fly fishing with all the cloud cover we are likely to see. So despite a few minor inconveniences, it's still a good time to fish the San Juan this week, and the small price we have to pay for a minor disruption in our normal fishing habits, will be well worth it, once all the work is done.

11/6/2011

Forgive me if I ramble here, but I've been trying to fill a deer tag, rising each morning well before dawn, then back to the shop for work by mid-day till way past dark-thirty. The sleep deprivation is beginning to take its cumulative toll on my lucidity and the hunting isn't going so well, either. Two mornings of sitting in below freezing temperatures with neither hide nor horn in sight. Out of sheer boredom this morning I nearly squeezed off a round at a coyote near my stand, but being the good natured soul that I am, I gave him a pass. If he shows up again tomorrow, he may not be so lucky, those song dogs aren't really known for their deer attractant qualities. Hopefully, I can get this business taken care of soon and start sleeping in a little and focusing more on my fishing. Although the weather has taken an abrupt turn towards winter, the fishing is still good here. It's just tough, going from 70 degrees one day, to a high of 35 the next, but it had to happen sooner or later. Supposedly, it will return to the mid 50's by Tuesday and throughout the rest of the week, so it should be plenty comfortable for a day on the water, and based on the lack of crowds, you won't have a lot of company. Last Tuesday the BOR dropped the water level to around 330 cfs without any adverse effect on the quality of fishing, other than opening up a lot more water that I can access by wading. In the upper river it's still the small midge game and you can find fish rising through the biggest part of the day. I know I said last week that I was going to devote an entire day to fishing streamers, but my success fishing dry flies on Monday, led me to do the same on Tuesday--old habits are hard to break. I began the day with my old standby the Fore and Aft in size 24 on 6X tippet, then switched over to an Olive Comparadun around 1:00 when the Blue Winged Olives started to come off and kept plenty busy until around 3:00 when they stopped. There were still plenty of midges on the water during the BWO hatch and enough fish rising to them, but I like using a larger fly I can see, like the Comparadun in size 22, if the fish are willing. After the BWOs stopped I decided to try a little experiment with the midge sippers and managed quite a few more fish on hopper and ant patterns, right up till dark, so that idea of fishing streamers went right out the window. I still plan to give it a go, but I'll have to wait for a day when there aren't so many fish rising, I just don't have that sort of discipline to abandon rising fish. If you like nymphing, don't worry, it's still an effective way to catch fish right now with midge larva, pupa, and emerger patterns, working well, especially from Texas Hole and above. With the increased activity of BWOs in the lower river, I wouldn't be without Fluff Baetis, Chocolate Foam Wings, and CDC Winged RS2s, if you target that area. So after a couple of cold, windy days with the snow and rain blowing sideways, we should be back to more acceptable weather for this time of year, and continued good fishing if you head out here this week. Now if I can just get those damn deer to cooperate.

11/11/2012

This coming week looks to bring us a lot of nice sunny days with highs around 50 degrees, which is some really comfortable fishing weather for mid- November in Northern New Mexico. The river is still fishing great; as it has for weeks, despite lower flows and the slight inconvenience of the stream restoration project that is taking place at this time. The work that is going on at this time has produced a few days of cloudy water downstream, but there's still plenty of water to fish, both in the area above the work and in the side channels below. Even at lower water levels, these side channels are holding lots of fish, and in fact they are easier to spot and fish to, under these conditions. The project itself; seems to be moving along well, and sources involved in the work have told me that they plan to finish their work in the river before their Dec. 15th deadline, possibly by the first of the month. We are still seeing good hatches of both midges and baetis, with lots of healthy, feeding fish taking advantage of the abundance of easily accessible food sources. Standard San Juan nymph rigs of small dark midge patterns have been good producers in the mornings, before the hatch comes off around 11:00 a.m. Once the hatch begins to pick up, switch from the pupa and larva imitations to emerger patterns and keep your weight small, as the flow is only around 330 cfs, and you don't need a lot of weight to sink size 24 to 26 flies, and get them down to the feeding lanes of fish. Once the fish start to focus on the adults, be prepared to switch it up to the midge dry patterns, like the Black Midge Adult, Griffith's Gnats, and Fore and Afts in sizes 24 to 26. 6x tippet for the nymphs and 7x for the dries, will help you take more fish, under the low clear water conditions, we are experiencing. Around 1:00p.m. start looking for the emergence of baetis, especially if you are fishing the lower section of the river. In fact, if I were fishing that area during this time of the year I would make a Chocolate or Grey Foam Wing, Fluff Baetis, or CDC Olive RS2, one of my fly choices, even if I didn't see the BWO's hatching. Once the baetis get going and the fish start keying in on them, my favorite fly is a CDC Olive Comparadun, with a dark grey wing. It's important to play close attention to what the fish are doing when these baetis are present. It usually takes quite some time, from the moment you start seeing the adult BWO's start appearing on the water, until the fish start actively feeding on them. If you're seeing only dorsal and caudal fins on the rise, don't jump the gun and make the switch to dries; just yet, your chances at taking fish during this time are going to greatly increase if you stick with those emerger patterns, with very little or no weight, and shorten up that indicator, in relation to your top fly. If you're really scrutinizing the type of rise that the fish are making, it'll be pretty easy to distinguish the point at which they begin to switch over to the adults. These rises are likely to be a lot less splashy, and will appear to be more of a sip, followed by a growing concentric ring on the water's surface, and usually you will only see the nose of the fish break the surface vs. the fins associated with emerger feeding behavior. I like to stop my activities from time to time when I start seeing the adults floating by and key in on a few bugs, watching their progress as they float downstream. Focus in on a particular insect and wait until you see several disappear under one of those dimples on the water, until you're committed to making the change to a dry fly pattern. Once you've detected this feeding behavior, try to pick out an individual fish that is rising with regularity and position yourself so that you won't be detected and can make the best drag fee presentation possible, into his feeding lane. With most of these San Juan fish; if they are feeding actively, you won't need to put your fly more than three feet or so in front of them, which will also help with having more line control and less drag on your fly, to be successful. I've also found that it helps to watch the fish long enough to determine his feeding pattern and try to time your cast accordingly, to put the fly in front of them at the opportune time. Generally, they won't and can't eat every bug that comes into their range and the usual pattern is rise, eat, drop to their lie, observe, pick out a target, rise again and eat. You'll need to calculate how long this takes for each individual fish and how long it takes for your drift to reach the fish at that precise moment of opportunity, but after a while it's a lot less harder than it sounds, and it becomes second nature for a good dry fly fisher. Hopefully, you'll get a chance to get out this week and experience this all for yourself, since no amount of writing; no matter how precise, can ever take the place of experiencing the real thing, when it happens for you on the river.

11/13/2011

Chaos Reigns! Order Must Be Restored! I had an uncle on my mom's side of the family that spent the majority of his adult life hunting, fishing, and trapping, much to the detriment of his normal housekeeping duties. On one occasion, after an evening hunt, he had a friend over for some venison stew and the friend remarked, "Your dog sure keeps looking at me awful funny." My uncle nonchalantly replied, "That's probably because you're eating out of his bowl." While my domestic situation hasn't quite deteriorated to that level yet, I must admit that the combination of two recent big game hunts and some stellar fishing conditions have left my domicile in such a sordid disarray of camo clothing, ammunition clips, backpacks, sleeping bags, muddy boots, rifles, and fly rods, that I have developed a genuine fear that I may be headed down that slippery slope towards household anarchy. Hopefully, my conge' to this final hunting season will spell the end of this domestic science reign-of -terror and I can ,once again, restore a semblance of order to this place, more akin to the type I experience when my life is more one-dimensional and my main focus is limited to fly-fishing, only. My motive for re-organization; at least to the level that I can find all my fishing equipment, could not be greater, with such unseasonably warm weather and numerous reports of great fishing that I have been hearing. To be honest, due to hunting season demands, and that other thing called "work", I've only managed a half day of steamer fishing over the past week and have been relegated to fishing vicariously through the reports of guides and other fishermen, passing through the shop. However, the half day I did pull off was stellar, and the reports have been good, as well. With the river flow around 370 cfs and clear water conditions, the possibilities for wade fishing have been outstanding with the ability to reach so many more spots in the river that were inaccessible at an 800 cfs flow. It has made things a little tougher for the drift boat guys, due to the slower current making for longer drift times between put-in and take-out points, and difficult navigation between wade fishermen now standing in areas they couldn't reach before, but it's all still very doable. Despite the numerous clear, bluebird skies we have been seeing, the midge and BWO hatches have been hanging in there, and the overlap of both have created favorable circumstances for hours of uninterrupted dry-fly fishing. In the words of Doc Holliday--"That's just my game." I was also very encouraged by the results from my half day of swinging olive wooly buggers and plan to revisit that tactic again his week. The nymphing game is still the same old tried and true tactics of small midge imitations in the upper river with baetis patterns prevailing in the lower stretches. With continued long term weather forecasts, it looks like we can look forward to more warm conditions, favorable to the outdoorsman, at least for the next ten days, or so. It would appear that the only change we could face in the near future that would affect the fishing dynamic would be the dreaded "lake-turnover." I've explained this natural occurring phenomenon in great detail; ad nauseam, in articles past, and it involves a lot of scientific mumbo-jumbo concerning thermocline inversion, water displacement, stratification, yada, yada, yada. Really, the only thing you need to know about it is that it happens here every year, usually between Thanksgiving and Christmas (depending on the weather) and it adversely affects the visibility in the river, and generally makes the fishing pretty crappy for a while. It varies both in duration and intensity from year to year and can affect the fishing for a week, up to a matter of months. I've seen it at its worst, which can make the water look like pea soup, and its best, which can cause a slight discoloration for a week or so, then clear up considerably. The main catalyst for it is cold weather that affects the upper layer of water temperatures in the lake, so it would appear that we should be spared for a while, given the weather we have been experiencing, which only gives you more reason to get out and fish now, while the conditions are so good. Hopefully, your holiday plans will include a little side trip to the San Juan to experience the great fishing we've been having, I know I'll be taking advantage of my extra day off on Thursday to spend some quality time on the water and I'm sure the housework can wait for another week.

11/18/2012

I received an e-mail recently from someone that fished the San Juan and the sender suggested that my fishing reports might be laced with hyperbole. I'll be the first to admit that none of my reports come with a money-back guarantee. However, I will also assert that I try each week to base these reports on my own personal experiences on the water, and those of skilled fishermen that know this river and fish it a lot, and I try to present them from an honest and objective viewpoint with as much veracity, as possible. I am going to draw the line on attaching that old advertiser's caveat, "your results may vary" to each one, but the reader must understand that these reports try to capture the most accurate up-to-the-moment snapshot I can provide with personal and garnered information, from what I feel are credible sources. So, I'm going to stand beside my claims that the fishing on the San Juan for the past several weeks, has been good, and that I expect that will continue, until the conditions change from outside source, such as the lake turning over or the weather taking any dramatic change. Hyperbole?; sorry, but I respectfully beg to differ from that opinion. I do promise that should the conditions and fishing quality change, I will try with all possible candor, to report that just as accurately. Now, as for what is happening out there now. Due to the recent good fortune of the continued nice weather, I have taken advantage of the warmer temperatures and have been getting on the water a little earlier than I am accustomed to for this time of year. By earlier, I mean 9:00 a.m. vs. 10:00 or 10:30. I'm seeing fish rising to midges as soon as I hit the water, and have been having good success fishing small midge dry patterns, and even getting away with using a size 20 Tav's Griffith's Gnat pattern. There may even be opportunities for this type of dry action at earlier hours, but I'm just not brave or desperate enough yet; to venture out there, until the sun is well on the water. I'm guessing here, but I would bet that 9:00 am is probably the beginning parameter for this hatch, since it's triggered mostly by water temperature and there's not that much sun on the water at this time of the year until around 9:00. I've been fishing this hatch until around 12:00, and as it tapers off, the baetis get going requiring a switch over to those patterns, which will keep you busy for a few hours more. It appears that the major concentration of the BWO's are now located from Simon Canyon and below, and the prolific hatches we were seeing in the Baetis Bend area seem to be tapering off. Fluff Baetis and Comparaduns are getting the job done in those areas. The weather for this week still looks good, with the possibility of some showers on both Mon. and Fri., but otherwise sunny with temperatures in the high 40's to 50 degrees. The stream restoration project in the Braids area is moving along nicely and David Israel from our shop who had a recent tour of the area with a DOW biologist, reports that they have done a nice job on creating some superb fish habitat, and even noting that there are trout moving into the newly created areas there. He added that it will probably take a while for the area to look a little more natural, but it seems the effect that they are after; which is creating better fish holding water in that area, is being accomplished. The flows are still around 300 cfs, due to the work being performed, but it doesn't seem to have affected the fishing much, and I caught some of my best fish last week, sipping midges in about a foot of water. I have been concentrating most of my efforts further downstream these days (Simon Canyon and below) and haven't really had an issue where I thought that the water clarity from the work became a problem. If the movement of the heavy equipment or the nature of the work changes enough to alter this pattern, there's still plenty of water in the Upper Flats to Cable Hole to keep me occupied. If you get the chance to get out this week, the weather and the fishing look to still be quite good for the San Juan, and if you feel the need to walk off some of that turkey and pumpkin pie, I can think of no better exercise that some water aerobics, wading the fine waters of this river.

11/20/2011

As the years pass and the remaining hair that I have turns a shade more toward salt than pepper, the passing thought that I will soon go the way of all flesh and someday leave this world seems to become more prevalent, with more time piling up behind me, than appearing ahead. I guess it's a natural way of thinking as we age, and maybe a good thing, if it increases the need to extract more enjoyment from the years ahead and the realization that the clock is ticking and time is a little more precious when it becomes a scarce commodity. Hopefully when the time comes, I can part in true fashion, as did Gilbert Pinchot, who was the first Chief of the U.S. Forest Service, former Governor of Pennsylvania and considered by most, the father of the conservation movement for this nation's natural resources. Gilbert spent a lot of his time in the field, preferring the beauty of the Cascade region and the company of the likes of his good friends Teddy Roosevelt and John Muir, to the stuffy government offices of Washington D.C. and Gilbert liked to fly-fish, sleep on the ground, under the stars, sit around a campfire, and blaze trails in the mountain regions of the American West. When he finally succumbed to leukemia at the age of 81, he was buried along with his favorite fly rod in Pike County, Pennsylvania. A class act, in both life and death. If, like Gilbert, you love the outdoors and fly-fishing, I can't think of a better time and place than The San Juan to pursue your passion. Unseasonable warm weather, sparse crowds, and lots and lots of fish are just the ticket for what ails you, and a welcome distraction from the sometimes twisted meaning that the Holiday Season can take on with the madness of such things as Black Friday and Cyber Monday. No matter what your method may be, nymphing, dry flies, or the streamer, it's all good right now. Winter flows are around the 400 cfs mark and are likely to remain there throughout the rest of this year and into the spring of the next. Water clarity is great, with no lake turnover, as of yet. The midge hatch starts around 10:00 am and goes on for the largest part of the day and is interspersed with some BWOs from around 1:30 till 3:00 on most parts of the lower river. The lower water level allows for more access to fishing spots that were inaccessible to the wading fisherman at the higher flows of 1,000 and 800 cfs, we saw throughout most of the summer and early fall. However, with the lower flows also comes slower current, which can translate to slower drifts and longer inspection times of your flies, by fish that seem to get a little more selective and discriminating each day. I spent Thanksgiving Day here on the water, as I always do, and started with good success tossing some size 24 gray Fore and Afts to rising fish in some moderate current. When it came time to move on, I spotted some big noses in a flat section of water ahead and decided to give those bigger boys a try. I managed to bring a few in the 17 to 18 inch range into the net, before the slight wind that now blows in the morning till around 11:00 went dead still. After that all I could manage from the bigger fish were a few heart stopping fly inspections, complete with a few nose touches, until I wizened up and went down to 7X tippet and a size 26 fly selection. These guys kept me busy for the next couple hours until some BWOs started showing up and more and more fish in different parts of the river began to rise. Now apparently the same switch that controls the BWO hatch is also wired into nature's wind speed, because every time I start to see these bugs, no matter how calm it is at the time, the wind invariably picks up and makes the casting, drifting, and seeing part of this fishing, harder. Nevertheless, I was able to get my CDC Comparadun in front of enough fish to keep me happy until the hatch ended, and then I switched back to midge patterns in the late afternoon and finished out the day with some more nice fish before it got just too dark to see anymore. I headed home with a smile on my face and hungrier than Alfred Packer and had my own version of a Thanksgiving Feast, compliments of a good friend that was kind enough to drop off several plates from their family get-together. As a side note, several people have asked me about avoiding all the little stockers that are out there right now and how to catch some bigger fish. The simplest answer I can think of and what works for me, is to stay away from those parts of the river where you are seeing heavy concentrations of these smaller fish (usually easily accessible places where the stocking truck can drive to) and to search out spots that are holding larger fish and sight fish to them. With the water as clear as it is and a good pair of polarized sunglasses it really isn't too hard to find the bigger fish right now. It also helps if you walk a little more slowly, take time to really look "into" the water, and get a higher perspective on the water, like the riverbank, or a protruding rock. Believe me, the big fish in this river haven't gone anywhere and if you want to catch them right now, it pays to walk a little and not just blind cast to the first piece of water you come to. My 2 cents for the week.

11/27/2011

Ham, salami, extra sharp cheddar cheese, mustard, on whole wheat, with barbecue potato chips, and washed down with cold clear water from my Nalgene bottle. That was my Thanksgiving feast, served streamside this past Thursday, and I couldn't have been more content with a 25 pound

Butterball, and a chilled bottle of fine Pouilly Fuisse. I had beautiful weather and was surrounded by rising fish, with not another soul in sight; I don't know how it could have been much better of a day. The first 30 minutes or so started a little slowly, but as the wind abated and as the temperature started to rise a bit, so did the fish. I fished until noon with a Tav's size 20 Griffith's Gnat, then switched to a number of different BWO dry patterns; all of which, produced fish, and finally settled with a size 22 CDC Comparadun, that seemed to work the best. I caught and released more fish than I can remember, in a long, long time, and stayed with it until the growling in my stomach and the fear of crossing back over the river to my car; in the dark, forced me to quit. As I drove toward home, the last bit of light from the late Fall sun, sinking over the western horizon, cast a brilliant orange glow over the distant hills, and a smile came over my face; as I thought, I truly have much to be thankful for. This coming week will bring a few changes to the fishing on the San Juan. For starters, the work on the Braids area is now finished, and after a walkthrough inspection with the project manager and members of the DOW, on Monday, the area is scheduled to reopen on Tuesday. Other than the planting of some grass in early March; that will hopefully have enough growth to stabilize much of the dirt work, before the high spring flows, it looks like everything is a go. I'm anxious to see the new water that this project has opened up, with some new deeper holes, added boulders and structure, and increased flows to the area above the Kiddie Hole. The diversion of the Rex Smith Wash from this area; to a settling area nearby, will be a welcome change to improve the silting problem that has existed there for quite some time. Secondly, it looks like they will kick up the flows from the reservoir to around 500 cfs on December 1st. The river has a lot of didymo and dead algae present right now, due to the lower flows and clear water conditions, and this increase will no doubt stir up a lot of that into the water for a few days, which will probably affect the visibility for a little while. I'm betting that this would be a good time to fish some red larva patterns and streamers for a few days, following the release. Once the lake turns over and the water clarity drops, this should help block some of the sunlight penetrating the water, and finish off the algae. This is probably not going to happen until we start getting some considerably colder weather. Speaking of weather, Monday through Wednesday, it looks like we will see warm temperatures in the low to mid 50's and then a chance of rain and perhaps a little snow, Thursday through Saturday, with the daytime highs dropping to around 40. I think the strategy for the week should be to stick with those midge patterns in the mornings, then go to the baetis around noon, for the first part of the week. After the flow goes up, try some brighter, bigger stuff and experiment a little with some streamers, especially anything in olive. Looks like an interesting week ahead, and the latter part of it could be a little challenging, but with a little adapting to the changing conditions, I think the fishing will be alright, especially after a day or so when the dust settles.

11/28/2012

Blue- Winged Olives, Baetis, Mayflies, BWOs, these are all terms used by most fisherman to describe the complex little insect commonly lumped together from the family Baetidae, genera Baetis, Diphetor and Ancentrella Plauditus and the family Ephemerellidae, genus Attenella. That is all a mouthful, and considering there are over 50 species within the Baetidae family alone, one could easily get lost in the entomological taxonomic specialization of a thing that can also be summed up as "trout food." Lucky for us is the fact that all these little buggers have a lot in common, especially when we consider their habits and how they relate to trout fishing. To begin with; although they exist in most western rivers throughout the year, their emergence stage which is generally throughout late fall to early spring, is of most importance to the fisherman, and thus, my focus on them here at this time, in a San Juan River fishing article. In general, they exist in 3 three stages: naiad (nymph), subimago (duns), and imago (spinner). The nymph is covered by a hard exoskeleton and maintains this juvenile stage of its life for about a year. During this time it lives on or beneath river rocks, feeding on diatoms and algae and moves in drifting currents with a flipping motion of its tail section to find new food sources, mainly during early morning and late evening hours. As fishermen we imitate this stage of the insects life with such patterns as pheasant tails, wd-40's, hare's ear's ,and fluff baetis patterns, and root-beer's to name a few. Later in life, nature comes calling and the need to procreate causes these nymphs to drift to the surface where they shed their skin in the surface film, and the dun crawls out. This is a particularly vulnerable stage for the bug and as it struggles to free itself from its exoskeleton, becomes a prime target for feeding trout that take advantage of its lack of mobility and becomes, as they say, "easy pickins." This stage is often imitated by emerger patterns like, CDC RS2s, foam wings, half-backs, Barr-emergers, soft hackles, and various "cripple" patterns that are out there. Once free from its nymphal shuck, the now emerged dun, floats on the surface as its wings dry, at the mercy of the current, and once again becomes the target of hungry fish. Although this highly exposed part of the insect's life generally exists for a matter of minutes, it is probably the most observed stage by fly fishermen, because of the bug's increased visibility, and thus the most "fished" part of the hatch. The most common imitations for the angler at this stage include sparkle duns, CDC comparaduns, and parachute baetis patterns. Eventually, the dun flies off, molts into the spinner stage, mates, and the females return to the water to lay eggs, and then die. This stage of the insect's life goes mostly unnoticed by many fishermen; due to the fact spinners lie flat on the water with their now translucent wings outspread and are difficult to see. However, trout target them in numbers, because they are, once again, easy targets. A dead bug isn't going to fly off anywhere. Often, rises from feeding trout during this time are mistakenly interpreted as rises to midges, since the spinners are more difficult to see, but the characteristic slow, subtle takes, of spinner rises, and the presence of swarms of mating spinners, higher above the surface, should be good clues to the fisherman that a spinner fall is in progress. Classic blue quill spinners and polywing imitations work as great imitations during this stage of the insect's life. Well, I know I have departed from my normal weekly format here, but maybe this was helpful to some and hopefully you'll get a chance to come out this week and put some of this into action. The midge and BWO hatches are still coming off, despite the sunny weather. The flows are still in the high 300 cfs range and the water clarity is good, although I noticed last week that it has just begun to turn a little bit.

Winter

4 WINTER

Fishing In Winter

Hues of brown and grey
Further darkening the rain glossed path
That leads to the slate, metallic sheen of the river

Distant walls of smoky, ominous clouds overhang
The distant buttes and mesas
Loneliness, a word that would soon pass for the feeling of solitude
Separating him from all other emotions

Thoughts reaching back
Forming the reasons for all that had brought him here
Feelings jumbled and tumbled together
Spun in a web, not so perfect as those
Of the spider beside him, in the winter willows
Their once brilliant green, now faded to yellow
In their winter dress

Cold wind against his face
And the calloused, weathered hands of too many years
Of doing just this

Longing to feel the connection of those
He so wistfully hoped, now still cared for him
Yet blissful in his self-inflicted pain
To rid him of an all consuming one that was stronger

The slightest dimple upon the water
He raises his rod tip, and all becomes
Once again, right with the world

12/4/2011

I have some good news, and some not-so-good news, for the fishing report on the San Juan, this week. First the good news, the Braids stream restoration project has been completed and that section of the river has been reopened, and by all accounts I have heard this week, it is fishing superbly. I haven't had the opportunity to fish it personally, but I have talked to a lot of people that have, and they have told me that the "new and improved' area is holding a lot of fish and that they are not that hard to catch. There seems to be a good mixture of some smaller (10 to 12 inch) fish, along with some (16 to 17 inchers) and a few fish over 20 inches, and most of the new runs and holes are holding a lot of them. As far as what to use, the choice of flies seems to run the gamut. Small stuff, big stuff, even reports of fish being caught on a number of different colored streamers, and cartoon hoppers. Some of the best reports I have heard are from those who have fished some larger than usual, San Juan patterns, like size 20 Tav's Big Macs, Abe's Midge Masters, and size 18 Red Midge Larva. A lot of the holes are 4 to 5 feet deep, and the current is a little stronger in there than before the construction, and some of the best results are coming from those that are fishing these spots with a little more weight than we are accustomed to at 500 cfs, so a number 6 split shot seems to be the best ticket to getting the flies down to the fish, and rigging your indicator to fish a little deeper. The rest of the river is fishing nicely, as well. There are still some good midge hatches from 10 a.m. to 12 p.m. and some decent baetis hatches from 12 p.m. till around 2:30, or 3 p.m., offering some good dry fly opportunities. Now, the not-so-good news. The weather for this week looks to be a little inhospitable for any would-be anglers. We have a little snow on the ground from the storm that moved in; over the last few days, and that's not really a big deal. However, the big change appears to be the drop in temperatures, starting on Monday, with the lows at night in the single digits and the highs in the first part of the week in the low 20's. Monday's forecast call for winds from 25 to 30 miles per hour, so that might be a good day to throw another log on the fire and stay inside and organize your fly boxes, tie some flies, or read a good book. From Wednesday, through the rest of the week we should see a little more sunshine, but the temps should only reach the low to mid 30's, which will be a little hard to take, after being spoiled with temps in the mid 50's for the last several weeks. It is winter in the Rockies, and we no doubt will have some more beautiful days with mild winter temperatures, before it's all over, but this week just doesn't look to be one of them. I've fished in much colder stuff than this, and caught plenty of fish, so outside of those high winds on Monday, the rest of the week is do-able, depending on your threshold for cold, and just how long you can stay cooped up inside, when you know there are lots of feeding fish out there.

12/8/2012

One of the guides here in the shop commented that my fishing reports always seem to reflect the good parts of fishing and seem to leave out those parts like falling in the river, or snagging your fly in the willows. In an effort to be fair to all, I must admit that I have and continue to have, my fair share of run-ins with Murphy's Laws Of The River. You know, those axioms of fly-fishing like: You've finally figured what they're taking, but you just broke off the last one in your box, on that last fish. No matter where you decide to cross the river, the last two steps to the far bank are always over your waders. Your worst tangle of the entire day will come when there are rising fish all around you and it's just a slight bit too dark to re-tie. That one final falsecast will always land in the top of the highest tree around. And always, no matter how calm it is, the wind will always, always start blowing, when the hatch starts and you tie on a dry fly. There are oh so many more, but due to the brevity of this article, I'll limit them to the few mentioned above. Now that we've gotten that out of the way, let's talk about San Juan fishing for this upcoming week. For starters, it's gonna get cold, especially during the first part of the week. The kind of cold that calls for knocking ice out of your guides, cold. The kind of cold that makes you wonder if maybe there is something more important you need to take care of, rather than fish on that particular day. Fortunately for me, I have a Scots-Irish heritage, which means I am stubborn and probably won't come up with a reason not to go out. It also means I like to have a little drink now and then, but I'm just too cheap to buy it, for myself. Anyway, you can expect to see the midge activity pick up around 10:30 or so and you can have some good results on small midge dry patterns for a few hours. The late evening midge hatches we were seeing when the weather was a bit warmer, don't seem to be as prevalent as before and the fish that are rising during that time seem to be few and really spread out. The BWOs haven't really been out in numbers lately, but with the change in weather we are expecting that could possibly change, so bring some comparaduns, or sparkle duns it you decide to come out. When you are not seeing surface activity, red and cream larva are good choices for you nymph rigs and grey and chocolate foam wings are working, as well. I did have to work a little harder than I have been accustomed to for my fish this past week, but I would still rate the experience as good to very good, overall. The water level is still around the mid 300 cfs level and the clarity is still very good, with no lake turnover yet. This translates to some slow moving currents in lots of parts of the river and makes the fish somewhat picky eaters, due to the fact they have a long time to look at your offerings, so I've gone to 7x for my dries, and it seems to have helped. You do need to be on your game for the ones that you can coerce to eat, because just like a good soufflé, they won't rise twice. Well, looks like I need to go digging through the closet for some more layers,

Monday will be here before you know it. Hope you can make it out and if you need to book a guided trip, room accommodations, or more info, give us a call at 505-632-2194. A special shout-out to Clayton Gist who was out again this week from Tennessee, it's always a pleasure swapping stories with you.

12/11/2011

"A clever cat eats cheese, then breathes down a rat hole, with baited breath"—W. C. Fields. For those of you waiting to see what this week's forecast for fishing on the San Juan will be, here is my prediction. It's probably going to continue to fish well for this coming week, but you may have a little weather to deal with. It looks like we may get rain and snow, every day except Thursday and Friday. The good part of the weather news is that it's not going to be as cold as the early part of last week and we should see mid to high 30's, most days. I had some really good fishing in the new Braids area, last Tuesday, but the high for that day only reached around 27 degrees, and I had forgotten how much I really dislike fishing with gloves on, or having to deal with ice in my guides, every third cast. Still I caught fish; in what seemed to me, brand new water, and went home cold, but happy. I am becoming a big fan of this new area; and after spending the bigger part of the day in there, only realized that I had not even touched many of the holes that they have created, until I started to find them by accident, stumbling out to the parking lot in near darkness. There's something for everyone in there. Some deeper, slower runs, some shallower faster ones, lots of boulders, logs, and even a beaver pond for some dry fly action. I'm anxious to get back out there and explore some more, and maybe try to cover a little more water next time, hopefully I'll have a little more self discipline to do so, I have a hard time moving on to new water when I'm catching fish, where I'm at. There are some spots with some big healthy fish and others just loaded with stockers, that will eat almost anything you throw at them; but overall, just good fishing in very fishy looking water. The best results seem to be coming from size 18 Red Larva and small grey and orange scuds and larger dark midge patterns like Tav's Big Mac and Abe's Midgemaster.

As for the rest of the river, the overcast days we are likely to see this week could bring on some good baetis hatches, so keep a good lookout for that to happen from 12:00 on, in the lower river. I had a report from some guys that were on the lake a few days ago chasing pike, and they told me that the lake is beginning to turn over and is becoming cloudy, but as of today, it has not affected the clarity of the river yet. Unfortunately, it's inevitable that this has to happen each year, but it's about that time again. Maybe we will be blessed again this year; like last, and it will be short in duration. But, right now it's still crystal clear, so I'm going to make the best of it while I can.

12/16/2012

Outside, icicles hang from my roof, snow covers the ground and dots the buttes that offer a backdrop for the slate colored river and dark, low hanging clouds, diffuse what little bit of light the sun has to offer for this time of year. It even looks cold. Trying times that test the mettle and dedication of a fly fisherman. Beneath the surface of the water, trout, both small and large, go about their daily routine, eating, resting, and defending their territory, with little regard for the seasonal change above. Living in a tailwater where the year-round water temperature rarely fluctuates, they could care less that you're bundled up like "Ralphie" from "A Christmas Story", awkwardly fumbling with your gloves, trying to tie on size 24 midges with stiff, frozen fingers. And so it goes, the battle continues for the faithful, neither snow, nor sleet, nor dark of winter, will keep us from our appointed rounds. Is it really worth it? Apparently for myself and a few other hardy, fleece and goose down encased souls, the answer is, yes. Looking at the 10 day weather forecast, the early part of the week will be one of those times to see how bad you really want a piece of this, with the high for three of those days failing to pass the above freezing mark. Wednesday shows a low of 3 degrees and a high of 25, a time that offers solitude on a river that can sometimes get a little crowded, but then, there's a reason for that. Thursday through the weekend, looks a little better, if you're planning a trip, there's sunshine and 40 degree temperatures ahead. The fishing is still good right now. The flows are around 350 cfs, with good water clarity and midge hatches, sprinkled with a few BWOs during the mid part of the day. I've been limiting my excursions to the hours between 11:00 am to 4:00 pm and fishing dry flies to lots of rising fish, partly because that's when that type of thing is going on, but also because it's the warmest part of the day. I've had my best success on size 24 Fore and Afts and Tav's Griffith's Gnats. Around 1:00, when I start to see a few Baetis on the water, I've been switching to a size 22 olive Comparadun and taking several fish, until that hatch dies off. If you're nymphing, red and cream larva are hard to beat for choices right now and grey and chocolate Foam Wings, along with Fluff Baetis and CDC RS2s, for areas below Texas Hole. I have also been hearing good reports on dead drifting Bunny Leeches in olive, brown, and grey, with an egg pattern or red larva as a trailer. That, no doubt, is a fun way to fish, when the trout cooperate and there is no mistaking the take, when they decide to eat it. Just a final tip before I go—I have noticed lately that the angle of the winter sun seems to produce a reflective glare from the surrounding canyon walls, making it nearly impossible to see a dry fly on the golden sheen it creates on the water's surface—Try moving to the opposite side of the river and face back into the sun for better visibility. It also helps if you position yourself, so you're looking slightly across and downstream at your fly. Hope you decide to come out and brave the elements with me this week.

12/18/2011

I'm beginning to think that there is some vast conspiracy with the weather here, lately. I'm having a hard time understanding how we can have such beautiful weather during the rest of the week, but it always seems to rain and snow and get colder on my days off. I guess I can take some consolation that the fishing has still been good and the weather could be worse; but that's still hard to take while I sit here gazing out the window at blue sky, no wind and temperatures in the 50's, knowing that tomorrow will bring cold rain and snow and the high will be in the low 30's. It looks like we'll get a little break on Wednesday, then Thursday and Friday will be a little rough, and Saturday and Sunday will be cold, but sunny. But hey it's winter, what are you gonna do? The fishing out here has been worth braving the elements for, lately. I spent a great day; again last week, fishing the new "Braids' section and even managed enough self discipline to move around a little more and see more of what this "new and improved" section had to offer. I walked away impressed. There are lots of neat little holes and short runs in there and most of them hold a lot of fish. To me, this section fishes like no other part of the San Juan, and reminds me more of fishing some of the freestone rivers I have fished, "pocket-water", some like to call it. Most of the runs are short, with some abrupt drop-offs, added boulder and log structures, and a few little funky little back eddies, thrown in for good measure, so they take a little work and some head scratching to get dialed in on the fish. Once you've got that mastered, you can move on to the next hole and start all over again; since few of these are one size fits all for your set up. I tried a lot of different fly patterns, but it seemed that the only one I could get consistent results on was a size 18 red midge larva. One other thing I discovered was that I had to use a little more weight than I was accustomed to for the San Juan, due to the quick drop-offs and short, deep runs. Be prepared to move that strike indicator around a bit, if you move from place to place. The rest of the river is fishing well, too. I spent the next day a little farther down river and had a wonderful time catching rising fish all day on a size 24 Fore and Aft, so it really depends on which type of fishing you prefer; but, right now the San Juan is offering some great opportunities for those that like winter-time fishing for trout. As for me, I'm just hoping that I can break this spell that this weather seems to hold over my days off. If not, maybe I can find some solace in the fact that it really, truly, could be worse. Either way, I know exactly where I'll be on the next day I don't have to work.

12/24/2012

Sometime during the night, this past week, in a flu and fever induced, half lucid state, I remembered having the vision of long, concentric, loops of flyline. Tight, arrow straight, u-shaped loops, like my old friend and former fishing partner, Andrew, used to throw. He's always been a better caster than I will ever be, one of those true naturals that make the process graceful and effortless, more art, than science. He says I play fish better than he does; to which I say, only shows part of his magnanimous spirit, the sort one desires in a fishing partner. Although work and life have put a lot of miles between us in the past few years, we still manage to fish together occasionally and the comfort level of an old friendship returns as naturally and effortlessly as those loops in my dreams. Since he moved on to another state, another career, and other waters, I fish mostly by myself these days. Calling just anyone you fish with on any particular day, a fishing partner, is like calling the best hunting dog you have ever owned, just another family pet. I get a kick out of some of the older guys that come into the shop from time to time, and you can immediately tell by the way they finish each other's jokes and stories, that they've no doubt, been fishing together for many years. Countless stories, countless places, and countless memories, concentric loops, life. This is going to be a tough week, weather-wise, for fishing the San Juan. The extended weather forecast calls for highs in the 20's, with some scattered snow throughout the week. The water level is still around 350 cfs, with mostly clear conditions. Midge patterns in sizes 24 through 28 are the major producers, right now, with the hatches occurring during the mid-day hours, between 11:00 am and 3:00 pm. There is still some Baetis activity around 1:00 pm till 3:00 pm on most days, on the lower river, and these upcoming overcast days should be a good time to target some fish with Comparaduns and Sparkle Duns. Next week looks to be slightly more user friendly, with daytime highs in the low to mid 40's. Whether it's this week or next, the fishing part of your trip is likely to be good and you're likely to find some solitude here if that's what you seek.

12/26/2011

Colder temperatures, lighter hatches, lower light levels, cloudier water, and less hours to get it all done in, should all combine for enough reasons to keep a guy at home and forego the sport of winter fishing in favor of more comfortable pursuits, within the confines of a warm home. But for those who love the sport and seek the solitude that this season offers, that's not likely to happen. To be honest, the fishing here has gotten a little tougher lately. While tailwaters like the San Juan can offer more predictable fishing this time of the year than those of the freestone variety, with more stable water temperatures and predictable bug activity, they do not come without winter challenges. One issue you are likely to face is that of lake turnover. This phenomenon occurs each winter on large deep bodies of water when the outside air temperature drops, cooling the upper layer of the lake (called the epilimnion). As this layer cools, it eventually becomes cold and heavy enough to cause it to sink, passing through the next layer (called the thermocline) and onward to the lowest layer; or hypolimnion, displacing this water at the bottom of the lake to the surface, mixing with the less oxygenated water on the bottom along with decayed vegetative matter, thus increasing the turbidity of the water. The end result of it all, is cloudier water being released into the river, making it tougher to spot fish, and tougher for fish to spot your flies. I have seen this event last anywhere to a few weeks, to months; here, and the clarity of the water to range from a little cloudy, to more like pea soup. Fortunately, since this occurrence started last week we have only seen the visibility decrease down to about two feet or so, which makes for a little tougher fishing, but overall not so bad for this time of the year. While opportunities for dry fly fishing still exist during this time, they have become more limited in scope, with small midge patterns like the Fore and Aft, working best between the hours of 12:00 to 300 p.m., in the slower water tailouts, below major riffles. There have been some baetis hatches in the lower stretches of the river lately, but they are sparse and short lived, and I have found the adults to go largely unnoticed, by most of the fish. For now; except those times when the fish are visibly on the midge feed, I would concentrate on the long pool stretches of the flats, where the winter-lethargic trout like to hold and expend less energy, and let the food come to them. Focus your efforts on the thalweg; or dominant area of current in the pool, that carries the highest concentration of food, to waiting trout. Bright and larger midge larva patterns like red midge larva, princess nymphs, and desert storms, in size 18 have been working well. You'll need to bring your A game and really work on getting your drifts just right and be ready for subtle takes, due to the fact that these winter fish don't typically move a lot and expend valuable energy to take a fly. Nonetheless; although challenging, these winter days still offer the chance to get out on the water without a lot of company and keep the "shack nasties" at bay.

12/31/2012

Occasionally, there's a little wisdom in all those hillbilly colloquial phrases that are somehow stuck in my noggin'. Take for instance, the one that says--"you've got a long row to hoe." That one in particular comes to mind when I think about how much more of these winter conditions we are going to have to endure, before we see some warm weather fishing. Now I know that there are certain positive attributes to wintertime fishing, like solitude, and the beauty of fresh, fallen snow, but those get a little harder to appreciate, when your mind starts wandering and you start looking off in the distance toward spring. When I was a much younger man, I always seemed to end up with a girlfriend, whose father owned a large farm. I don't know how this always happened; maybe I unconsciously became my own worst enemy--placing too much belief in all those old "farmer's daughter stories", of my youth. Whatever the case, come the hottest part of summer, I invariably found myself, with a farm implement in my hands, staring down a seemingly, endless row of tobacco plants, wondering how I got there and thinking that "I've got a long row to hoe." I guess the good news in all of it, was that no matter how endless they seemed, there was always an eventual end to those long, long, rows and also that those "farmer's daughter stories", also bore out a little truth, as well. So for those of you who prefer to do your fishing in short sleeves, rather than layers of fleece and gloves, hang in there. I know it looks like one of those long rows, but before you know it, we'll be through January and on to February (which is the shortest month of the year), and into March; which can be considered spring in most cases, and we'll be home free, with winter all behind us. In the meantime, there's some days, where we're just gonna have to slog it out, so if you decide to give it a go in the near future, you can get some pretty good results out there with an egg pattern, teamed up with a red larva imitation. Streamer patterns of olive and brown are working well, also, and make a good fly choice on those particularly cold days, when rigging small nymph patterns, become troublesome for cold fingers. Although the water clarity has decreased somewhat in the last week or so, there are still dry fly opportunities on midge patterns like the Fore and Aft and Griffith's Gnats, during the midday hours. So, not to worry, we'll get through this. There's gonna be some be some tolerable weather in the near future, in the meantime, my advice is to just keep your head down and keep hoeing and try not to focus so much on the end of the row.